I HAVE SEEN GOD

I HAVE SEEN GOD

The miraculous story
of the Diospi Suyana Hospital in Peru

Klaus-Dieter John

MONARCH
BOOKS

Oxford, UK & Grand Rapids, Michigan, USA

Published by Monarch Books
an imprint of
Lion Hudson plc
Wilkinson House, Jordan Hill Road,
Oxford OX2 8DR, England
Email: monarch@lionhudson.com
www.lionhudson.com/monarch

ISBN 978 0 85721 574 1
e-ISBN 978 0 85721 575 8

Original edition published as *Ich habe Gott gesehen* by Brunnen Verlag
GmbH

This edition 2014

A catalogue record for this book is available from the British Library

Printed and bound in the UK, August 2014, LH26

To you, Tina:

For more than thirty years, you have shared in

the writing

of every one of these pages

Contents

Foreword

I cannot ever remember reading a book that brought tears to my eyes. But when I read Dr Klaus John's book, I was profoundly moved and occasionally struggled to read the pages through misty eyes. While some books can inform or entertain, this book can change the way you see the world and transform your understanding of the meaning and significance of life. My hope is that as you read the story of Diospi Suyana, you will discover a new perspective on the sacredness of life and the transforming power of Christian compassion.

First published in Germany in 2010, the book has become a bestseller and is already in its seventh edition. I predict that this book and the incredible story it narrates may well become a sensation in the English-speaking world. The story of the miraculous events that led to the hospital's founding is deeply moving and the style of writing is lucid and compelling throughout.

Diospi Suyana is from the Quechua language and means, "We trust in God". Although the author is unapologetically Christian and his faith perspective is apparent throughout, my hope is that people of all faiths and none will be able to read this book and be inspired and encouraged by the vision, warmth, humour, humanity, and compassion that exude from every page.

I have to admit to being somewhat sceptical when I first heard about the story of Diospi Suyana. I thought it was going to be just another one of those typical missionary stories that makes grandiose claims about "miracles", but which appear to lack credibility and, on closer inspection, turn out to be rather insipid events for which there are perfectly rational explanations. But Klaus refers to "miracle" as a series of events that defies any kind of logical explanation or human expectation. Moreover, at a deeper level, he uses the term to evoke the value, sanctity, and dignity of human life and encourages us to think of life itself as the greatest miracle of all.

Klaus' story evokes memories of the German-French philosopher and doctor, Albert Schweitzer. Abandoning a glittering career as a well-paid philosophy professor and leading thinker of his time, Schweitzer decided in 1905, at the age of 30, to devote his life to serving the poor as a medical doctor in Africa.

One of the reasons why I admire Klaus and Martina John is because, like Albert and Helene Schweitzer, they discovered from an early age their life's project and pursued it in faith and trust. From the mustard seed of a vision and a prayer, there has developed a thriving community of grace planted in Peru in the form of a missionary hospital.

Through their work hundreds of thousands of lives have been irreversibly transformed for the good. I therefore read the story of Diospi Suyana as a blessing and inspiration, but also as a challenge.

Dr Joshua Searle
Spurgeon's College, London

Introduction

The book you are now holding was published in German in 2010, and turned out to be a bestseller. A few months after publication, on July 30, 2010, I was sitting at my desk at the hospital just letting my mind wander when I was suddenly struck by the thought that it would be a good idea to make the story accessible to an English readership. My thoughts turned to Janet Yachoua, a kind English lady who had been living in Wiesbaden, a town near Frankfurt, for over twenty-five years. She runs her own translation office and had translated items into English for our website on several occasions in the past. I sent her an email, hesitantly inquiring whether she had heard of the book and, if so, whether she felt she could possibly help with translating it. You could have knocked me down with a feather when the reply came the next day: "Believe it or not, I was just thinking yesterday about translating the book, and spent some time praying for you... a couple of hours later you emailed me – sounds like a divine plan :-) When do you need it? Janet."

I had not had much contact with Janet over the previous two years but she did know the book; in fact, it had been sitting on her desk for a while waiting for the friend she had bought it for to return from holiday. At exactly the moment when I was in the Peruvian Andes carefully wording my email to Janet, she was looking at the book and experienced an inner calling to translate it.

Over the next two months she painstakingly translated the entire book into English. The text was then revised by Jennifer Baldwin for an American audience. This English "original" was the basis for the Spanish version, the youth edition in several different languages, and the book you are holding in your hands at this moment.

I´d like to add that Janet would not accept any payment for this mammoth task.

If you would like to know how Janet got hooked on this story of providence and wonders, just keep reading... people have been known to read it in one sitting through the night.

1

On the Brink of Death

Fog clothed the hairpin bends with an impenetrable shroud of white as I carefully maneuvered my vehicle around the endless curves of the mountain pass.

David Brady and I were returning from yet another meeting with government representatives of the Abancay Province in central Peru. It looked as if our persistence had finally paid off – the authorities had agreed to begin paving the access road to our mission hospital soon.

Unfortunately, we could not always avoid making this dangerous trip at night, and every now and then we were met by the hazy flicker of the lights of oncoming vehicles. I wiped the windshield with my hand and gave David a sober look.

"It's going to take us an hour longer to get to Curahuasi in this weather," I said sullenly. We had long since left the treeline behind and would reach the pass in a few minutes.

Glaring headlights sped towards us. The vague outline of a tractor trailer left the inside bend ahead of us and suddenly loomed large. Something was very wrong. The truck's lights had already passed us, but something dark was flying at us, completely blocking the way. Instinctively, I jerked my 4x4 over onto the far side of the lane. I was familiar with every inch of that road and knew all too well that, just beyond the asphalt edge, there was a deep and deadly drop.

We hit the trailer hard. I took a heavy blow to my left side. Splinters of glass rained into the vehicle, covering the interior. The screech of twisting metal reached my ears but seemed to be coming from miles away. Then all was quiet. But my car was still spinning uncontrollably towards the bushes – and the dreaded edge. David Brady sat motionless beside me. The eternity of a few seconds passed. Then, without knowing whether or not I was even conscious, David cried out the command that saved us: "Brake, Klaus!"

My right foot slammed down on the pedal. Our vehicle came to a halt on the very brink of the precipice. We had survived. In fact, we had escaped death twice within seconds – a different angle of impact during the collision or a plunge into the depths would have left two widows and six fatherless children.

There we stood, at the site of the accident – 11,000 feet up in the mountains, in the drizzling rain and the darkness of night. In disbelief, I stared at the pile of junk in front of me, from which I had just managed to climb via the passenger side. The car was completely destroyed, yet I had only a sore shoulder and a trickle of blood on my left cheek.

Somewhat later I thought that God must surely have had His reasons for sparing our lives on the night of December 16, 2008. Maybe one of them was so that we could share the story of Diospi Suyana.

2

High-School Sweethearts – For Life

I fidgeted restlessly in my chair. Out of the corner of my eye, I surveyed the classroom: there *she* was. As usual, she was deep in conversation with the girl next to her. She had been attending the Elly Heuss High School in Wiesbaden for six and a half years, just like me, but somehow I had never noticed her before now. Prior to this year – our senior year – our paths had seldom crossed. Now I found myself in not one but seven courses with this attractive girl – all in the close quarters of a 270-square-foot classroom.

Even more than her beautiful blue eyes, which undid me with just a glance, it was her soft, gentle voice that had me completely under its spell. At seventeen years of age, I had heard thousands of voices, of all types and timbres. But this one was different – alluring, quiet, seductive. As the student representative for the school, I was used to public speaking; perhaps I even liked the sound of my own voice too much. When this girl spoke, however, I held my tongue and hung on to her every word.

This charming young lady was clearly the pulsating heart of a large group of girls. An attentive observer, I had worked that out fast. Whether she was out riding a horse belonging to local business people in the afternoon or making the rounds of all the coolest clubs with her friends in the evening, it was always the same – the intimate details of all her leisure activities had been discussed in detail with the other girls by the end of the sixth period. Her world was totally different from mine.

I came from a family of hard-working bakers. From 2 a.m. until the evening news came on the radio at 7 p.m., they labored tirelessly in their bakery. Having first-hand experience of hardship and loss, they undoubtedly felt an overwhelming need to provide for themselves and their four children. My mother, Wanda, had been deported from Pomerania. My father, Rudolf, was an escaped prisoner of war from Silesia. Their roots in Eastern Europe, the sufferings of war, and finally the blossoming of love had bonded the two in a common destiny. But it was their faith in God that truly made them one.

Our Sunday mornings were always spent at the Baptist church, which we lovingly dubbed "the chapel." As a boy I found the services long, but never boring. I was admittedly often preoccupied by the pretty stained glass on the ceiling or the facial expressions of the other worshipers, but some of what was said somehow made its way into my heart.

I loved it when missionaries came to tell us their stories and show us pictures from "the field." I imagined I was right there with them, climbing into a hand-carved log boat to cross the dangerous currents of the Amazon River. I dreamed of owning a station wagon one day, just like the ones the missionaries used to cross the African savannah. Every slide projected onto the wall promised adventure and excitement in exotic lands.

At night in bed, I used to read stories by the "Jungle Doctor," Paul White. This general practitioner from Australia spent two years of his busy career in the endless expanses of Tanzania. Then, as if a doctor had nothing better to do, he wrote adventure stories for children and young people. The doctor under the baobab tree could not have known the impact the reports of his experiences would have on me. His books filled my imagination with the mysterious figures of unfathomable Africa. It all captured my attention far more than day-to-day life in Wiesbaden, a medium-sized city in Germany, in the 1960s.

My parents had chosen not to have a TV simply because of lack of time. During recess, when my classmates talked about the latest film or jokes heard on TV the night before, I had nothing to contribute. My time would come in class when the teacher told us about foreign lands, cultures, and explorers. This was a world I knew, and in which I somehow felt I belonged.

Back in the classroom, I slowly approached this feminine creature as if guided by an invisible hand. A moment of great revelation came during one of our very first conversations – I could scarcely believe what the girl with the blue eyes had just told me: "After I graduate, I want to study medicine and then work in a Third-World country." Even back in the eighth grade she was passionate about her unusual dream, and wrote extensively about it for a school essay.

"That's exactly what I want to do too," I replied, trying hard to sound casual. I took an even closer look at the pretty face beside me. Could it be that it was no coincidence our paths had crossed? Would my innermost longings be fulfilled with this whirlwind at my side? A quiet assurance began to stir, and deep within me I knew that this was the girl I would one day marry: Martina Schenk, a young woman full of life and passion, with the same fervent determination that was in me.

3

To Ghana and Back in Six Weeks

After the summer of 1978, our paths were never to diverge again. We did break off our "friendship" officially more than once, but somehow the two of us were just always together. We co-led a youth group, attended the same church, were active in the peace movement, and even had the same friends. And, of course, we were studying medicine together at the Johannes-Gutenberg University in Mainz. Our conversations were often about our future work as doctors in a developing country. This is actually not unusual – many medical students talk about doing this. But after their studies are completed, reality usually sets in. They often start a family, pursue further training in their specializations, buy a house, etc. The order in which these activities occur may differ, but the result is the same – these doctors stay at home.

German students of medicine have to provide proof of supervised practical work experience in hospitals. This "internship" period is very popular with medical students, as it gives them an opportunity to check out the "real" working world, and it often serves as a first step in securing future employment in the field.

Martina's parents were not the only ones who were shocked when she announced in the spring of 1983 that she was going to do her internship in Ghana, of all places. Her decision was probably influenced by a student from Ghana named Chris Sackey. He was a massive black guy who had enrolled in a school in Mainz to study economics. He rather self-confidently claimed the title of advisor to the government in Accra, and presumably really did have a variety of contacts there.

Chris seemed like a pretty nice guy, if somewhat lacking in transparency. As it turned out, he was the uncontested leader of a gang, and occasionally supplemented his meager income by smuggling gold across the Ghanaian border. There was considerable political turmoil in Ghana at this time, but Chris did not see it as an obstacle to Tina's projected visit to his homeland. Even the failed coup against dictator Jerry Rawlings and the state of emergency that was declared two weeks before Tina's scheduled departure were not regarded by Chris as problems that would preclude travel.

Maybe Martina felt that stepping out into the big, wide world was a bit risky – at least alone. When she asked me if I would go with her, I agreed immediately. We weren't technically "together" at this point, but we made a good team for this dicey business.

Soon we were only a few days away from the first great adventure of our lives. A former Third-World aid worker recommended that we visit Dr. Marquard, a Catholic doctor in Tübingen who had worked in Ghana for a quarter of a century. During our visit, Dr. Marquard served us bread and hot tea, and gave us a couple of boxes of malaria tablets. As we were leaving, she read us a few verses from Psalm 91: "A thousand may fall at your side, ten thousand at your right hand, but it will not come near you." She could not have chosen a better verse for us, for even though we played the part of intrepid adventurers, deep down we were more than a little apprehensive.

Our Aeroflot flight took us via Moscow, Odessa, and Tripoli to Accra, the capital of Ghana. To be on the safe side, we had stuffed our backpacks full of canned food and long-life cheese. We were thus armed against the famine ravaging the land – unless, of course, our food was stolen.

Somewhat hesitantly, we stepped off the plane into the heat and humidity of West Africa. A look around the airport did nothing to inspire confidence. A sea of unfamiliar and curious faces stood before us like a dark wall.

We moved cautiously but deliberately towards the airport exit and the reality of a so-called Third-World country. We had always been quick to claim that we wanted to spend our lives working with the poor, and now here we were. Regardless of the outcome of our present "experiment," in six weeks we would be on a plane back to the safety of Germany.

"Hey, here I am!" a tall man called from the confusion of the crowd. Chris Sackey had promised to meet us at the airport, and he was as good as his word. Interestingly, Martina's letter to him about our travel details had never actually left Accra's Central Post Office, yet somehow Chris had managed to fish her letter out of a mailbag so that he knew what time to meet us.

If the realization that Africa was different from Germany had not yet hit us, it certainly did when we attempted to use the airport restrooms. Every one of the toilet bowls was full to the brim with a stinking mush of excrement. Our disgust could have easily given us chronic constipation, but within two days we both had persistent diarrhea, which stayed with us until our departure.

Would Africa be the setting for our professional future?

Aghast, we regarded the nearly mile-long lines of empty vehicles at the gas stations. There was no gas. Drivers had simply given up hope of there ever being any, and subsequently abandoned their cars in endless rows. Wherever we looked, we saw beggars and crippled children on the ground. At a roadblock, we witnessed a soldier pointing his gun at an old man, forcing him to his knees. We were deeply relieved when no shot followed.

The Yeboah family's living room was the scene of lively conversations each evening. Another adventurous route had brought us to Kumasi, capital of the proud Ashantis, where Monika Yeboah, a native of Frankfurt, Germany, lived with her husband and six of her eight children. We directed countless questions to her: Why did we see so many men playing dice all day in the shade of trees while their wives were out laboring in the fields? Why did most of the men have concubines and mistresses? This was a very common practice, but obviously distressed the women greatly.

If not careful, one can very easily fall into the trap of racism in Africa. Even experienced aid workers and missionaries describe the African soul as unfathomable. Martina and I sucked on slices of orange and pondered for hours over Africa and her people. Perplexed, we wondered if we could ever feel at home in a society like this. It was difficult enough for us to distinguish one Ghanaian from another, but far more challenging to understand their nature.

The little we had seen so far of Africa seemed dark and threatening. Perhaps it had something to do with the unfamiliar, intense color of her people's skin. But even the city of Kumasi was wrapped in a cloak of blackness at night, with neither street lamps nor neon signs to shed even a faint glimmer of light. It was, after all, a city of 300,000 inhabitants, yet not in the least inviting. We were glad to forgo an evening stroll in the city. Besides, there was an enforced curfew which began at 6 p.m. each day. We were in no hurry to risk an encounter with armed men after what we had witnessed earlier from the military.

One afternoon, we lost track of time. We had gone to visit an American family, friends of Monika. When we noticed the length of the shadows, we realized that we were late and would never make it through the checkpoint before the curfew began. Monika was remarkably calm. We said a prayer for God's protection, and as we approached the security forces' barbed-wire barrier there was a sudden tropical downpour. All the soldiers fled from the road to seek shelter. We continued on our way without incident and reached the Yeboahs' home safely. Prayer being answered in such a dramatic and immediate fashion was something new for us. There was a nagging question of whether the downpour had just been an incredible coincidence, a whim of nature at just the right moment.

The weeks in Ghana turned out to be an eye-opening experience for us in every regard. At the large, municipal Komfo Anokye Teaching Hospital in Kumasi, there was an appalling lack of hygiene and organization. Upon entering the building we were struck by a strange odor, and soon afterwards learned that the hospital was infested with rats.

Monika Yeboah kindly arranged for us to do a two-week placement at a mission station at Lake Bosumtwi. As we climbed out of the station wagon when we arrived there, there was no question that we had reached the heart of Africa. Undulating hills surrounding the broad lake that would take at least a day to hike around, sleepy fishing villages comprised of round, straw-roofed huts lining the banks, the setting sun painting the sky in shades of red, and the dull pulse of drums floating out over the lake – a composite picture to transport us back to the time of Livingstone. The Africa described in children's books really came alive here. Here one could live in peace – if it were not for the constant chirping and buzzing of insects and the concomitant risk of malaria, a great concern for the Ghanaians.

The mission station was overseen by Margery, a Methodist nurse from England. She and her four Ghanaian assistants were treating between fifty and eighty patients a day. She was rock solid in every respect, fazed by nothing. The first time Tina contracted malaria, Margery remained calm and collected, stoically administering medication until Tina's glowing red face returned to its normal color.

As there were no good laboratory facilities, medical practice usually consisted of a visual diagnosis and the distribution of tablets. Standards at the pediatric hospital in Kumasi were not much higher. Dr. Hunter, an Indian, used to examine up to 200 young patients each morning. Spreading out his left hand, he would grasp the child's belly, simultaneously palpitating the liver with his fingers and the spleen with his thumb while using his right hand to write notes in the medical records. When we turned up one day at lunchtime, he told us what he was planning to do that afternoon.

"Now I need to get some paper, pencils, gas, and food. If you don't organize it yourself, you will have to manage without!" he advised.

Our experiences with the various regional medical facilities made one thing very clear to us fast – Ghana lacked just about everything we took for granted in Germany, and, as a result, medical standards were frighteningly low. Was there any point in having studied extensively for years in

25

Mainz, learning theory and state-of-the-art methods, only to come here and use none of it? The most disturbing thing was the indifferent, inhumane attitude of African society to suffering, even in state-run hospitals. If a patient could not pay the medical fees, he simply was not treated. In other words, if you don't have a wad of cash to give to the surgeon, you might have to take care of your infected appendix yourself.

Martina and I took stock of the situation. First of all, despite their shortcomings, the mission hospitals we had visited functioned far better than the state-run clinics. Secondly, we considered the Christian teaching about loving your neighbor to be more than just a cliché; it was to be reflected in the loving care of a doctor for a patient. We saw little sign of that in most places here. In short, the thought of working long-term in Ghana or a similar country was rapidly losing its appeal.

We were wondering whether to just ditch our plans to serve as missionary doctors when things suddenly took a remarkable turn. We made the acquaintance of Professor Dr. Eldryd Parry, a gaunt, rather serious physician from Wales, who proved to be the positive influence we had hoped to encounter during our internship in Ghana.

Not that he dispelled our misgivings with clever reasoning or patted us reassuringly on the shoulder: he did nothing of the sort. In fact, he said very little. Still, he was the incarnation of hope in the midst of injustice. Much to the sorrow of his family in Britain, he had left behind a promising career in order to help build up the Ghanaian healthcare system. Wherever he went, he was preceded by his noble reputation. "He even shared his last slice of bread with his gardener," some whispered. Others murmured, "He is a good example from head to toe."

Shortly before leaving Ghana, we spent the night at his home. As we drifted off to sleep, we heard him singing softly – not radio hits, but psalms from the Bible. The man had not allowed his unanswered questions to derail or defeat him. He drew his strength from his faith in God, a steady faith that seemed unaltered by mood swings or tumultuous circumstances. Professor Parry's life was a clear message to us, and he became one of our most significant role models.

4

My Mailbox Experience

A smile spread over my face as I quickly traced my fingers over the pages of the book. What I was holding in my hands was a real treasure trove. The catalog listed in alphabetical order all American universities that included a medical school. In the summer of 1984, there were 120 of them. Back then there was no internet with search engines that spat out information and addresses in a matter of seconds. When I learned of the catalog, I made a note of the publisher and ordered a copy by mail. A few weeks later, I had the information I had been seeking.

I had battled through to the eighth semester and was already thinking about where I might graduate. From talking to fellow students, I had gathered that training in the United States was more practical and therefore better than training in Germany. At some point I decided that I would complete my final two semesters in the USA.

Today there is nothing unusual about an exchange visit to another country. There are numerous political and educational organizations that facilitate this important cultural experience for students at multiple educational levels. The United States, Canada, New Zealand, Australia, and England have always been highly popular, but as recently as twenty-five years ago it was extremely difficult for a German student to be able to study

In another country – particularly in the USA. One reason for this was the hefty fees that American students were required to pay. A student exchange was further complicated by the fact that the educational systems were so completely different. In Germany, the final year of medical school consisted of three block placements: internal medicine, surgery, and a specialty practice elective. Each block lasted for four months.

Students could apply to the university teaching hospitals for these placements. Wistfully, I surveyed a map of the United States. How was I ever going to be able to put my plan into action? I did not have any close relationships with influential professors who had transatlantic contacts, nor could I speak English that well. The more information I gathered from the Dean's Office in Mainz, the less realistic my plans appeared.

What American university would accept me for four months when their own students were allowed to study elsewhere only for a maximum of eight weeks? The biggest hurdle of all turned out to be the German bureaucracy. "Either you find a university placement for four months, or you stay here!" The Dean's conditions were uncompromisingly stark.

I had to admit that my position was far from promising. Without a lot of help – from wherever – I would never get to the States. Confronted by my own limitations, I decided to ask for help from a different source: I began to pray. In January 1984, I began asking God each evening to guide me through the maze of logistical and bureaucratic challenges so that I might be able to study in the United States – providing, of course, that this was also His plan for me. I got very specific and asked God to take care of all the formalities by the first day of my medical graduate exams in August 1985. I still had plenty of time, and I faithfully prayed that same prayer every night.

The weeks and months passed. I completed an internship at the US Air Force Hospital in Wiesbaden to improve my English. The surgeon, a Texan named Dr. Locker, befriended me. But despite his hearty laugh, he could do nothing to cheer me up. I was consumed with anxious uncertainty. One day, during lunch in the cafeteria, I managed to knock over a full glass of milk. The pool of milk on the floor before the eyes of a much-amused crowd reflected how I felt – incompetent and totally overwhelmed.

In January 1985, I mustered all my courage and typed out my résumé – in English. Using a photocopier, I prepared application packets for forty different universities. With mixed feelings, I put them all in the mail and waited for what was to come. The countdown to my exams in eight months had begun.

For what seemed like an eternity, nothing happened. Absolutely nothing. Then the first refusals started to trickle in. "We regret we are not able to give you a positive response." "All of our places for visiting students are already taken." "Our educational system does not allow for a four-month training block." I carefully placed these and all other, similar, refusals in a file. The University of Wisconsin offered me a two-month training block in surgery. The University of Texas offered me an eight-week placement in gynecology, but it would not begin until the end of 1986. These two responses were a tiny flicker of light in the darkness, but were not actually much help. The door to America remained firmly closed.

Time passed. Winter became spring, spring became summer, and still I stood there empty-handed. My hope melted like butter in the sun. I dealt with my disappointment each evening with the same, almost stereotyped prayer: "God, if it is Your will – take me to America!"

It was July and my exams loomed. The heat was being turned up by the Dean's Office. "Please inform us immediately at which German teaching hospital you wish to complete your training," the secretary demanded. "Studying in the USA is obviously not going to happen!"

As I sat on my bed, I contemplated my situation. My own efforts in the past eight months had certainly come to nothing. My daily prayers over the last twenty months also seemed to have got me nowhere. I had been waiting and hoping in vain. The taste of defeat was indeed bitter. At this moment of absolute frustration, a daring thought passed through my mind: Ask God for an acceptance in tomorrow's mail!

I knelt by my bed and, in complete helplessness, I prayed, "God, if You are there and if it is Your will, send me an acceptance from the USA in the mail tomorrow!"

I was trembling with anticipation when I opened my mailbox at the usual time the next morning. There was a letter in there, and it was not difficult to recognize that it had come from the US. A stamp on the front indicated that it was from Case Western University in Cleveland, Ohio. I ripped open the envelope and unfolded the letter:

Mr. John,

We are pleased to inform you that we are able to offer you two months' training in surgery!

I was speechless! I translated each individual word twice, then three times, all with great care. No doubt about it – the famous Case Western Reserve had accepted me as a visiting student. After an internal prayer of thanks, I jumped into the car and drove straight to the university in Mainz. Professor

Löffelholz took a good look at the letter from America. He finally decided to grant an exception in my case and allow me to complete my surgical rotation at two different universities, one in Wisconsin, the other in Ohio.

The details of my final-year placements in internal medicine and specialty practice had not yet been worked out, but my "mailbox experience" had led me to an absolute assurance that God was with me. He would lead me and I could trust Him.

With this certainty, I promptly cancelled my registration at Mainz University.

It was ten days until the first four-day block of exams. God clearly needed to act, since apart from the four-month placement in surgery, I had nothing. Having separated from Mainz, I was like a skydiver who has jumped but not yet made a safe landing. However, my faith in God was stronger than ever. I was barely surprised to find a letter from the University of Virginia in my mailbox:

Dear Mr. John,

You may study Internal Medicine at our university for four months!

It was not until several months later, after my arrival, that I actually learned why the University Clinic in Richmond had made me this unusual offer.

"It was like this," one of the admin officers explained to me. "Each year, we take one student from Europe. Of course, over a hundred had applied for this one position, and it was just too difficult to make a decision. To be honest, I just stuck my hand into the pile of résumés and pulled one out at random!" I gulped. So *that* was what had happened.

On the first day of exams, I drove home exhausted, making a brief stop at my mailbox. A letter from the States smiled at me, and my heart began to race.

Dear Mr. John,

You may train in pediatrics at our university in Denver for three months.

Perfect! With the four weeks of vacation to which I was entitled, the acceptance from Denver solved what was left of the puzzle regarding my final year of medical studies in the US. God had answered three times, and within the timeline I had asked – to the very day. I began to realize that, with God at my side, the improbable and seemingly impossible could indeed become possible. I just had to do one thing: trust Him.

I bought a plane ticket, packed my two suitcases, and on October 25, 1985, I flew People's Express from Brussels to New Jersey. "Go west, young man!"

5

Zigzagging Through the States

In New York, I was reunited with my old school friend, Axel Peuker. His notable career as an economist had brought him to the World Bank there a year earlier. I was trying to recover from my first case of jet lag, lying on the couch in his attractive Manhattan apartment, drinking hot tea to revive my tired spirits.

In the evening, Axel showed me around the city, rightly called America's biggest melting pot. We took a ferry over to Long Island, and I turned up the collar of my fleece-lined leather jacket against the cool air. The crossing lasted only about fifteen minutes, but it was to have a profound effect on my thoughts, with serious consequences. Axel was a convinced atheist, highly intellectual and well-read. Our friendly conversation at the ship's railing challenged my faith in God for a significant period of time. Although I cannot remember the finer details of the conversation, a shadow of doubt was cast over the next thirteen years of my life. In my quiet moments, I was tormented by the fear that God was nothing more than a pious hope.

Beginning my studies at Case Western University in Cleveland was tough in every respect. I was assigned to a group of medical students who were doing their third year of training at Metropolitan Hospital. At 5 a.m. every day I crept through the tunnel that connected the nurses' dormitory, where my room was located, with the hospital itself. At 9 p.m., I dragged myself back through that tunnel, completely exhausted. Every third day I was assigned night duty and was on the ward or in the operating room without a break. My working week consisted of 120 grueling hours. During classroom training sessions, we students would often crash as soon as we sat down in the comfortable chairs. This did not seem to bother anyone. Our supervisor had been through the same rigorous training and understood first-hand that there is a limit to the demands one can make of a human body.

My English was improving and my self-confidence was growing visibly. Could I perhaps study at an American university as elite as, say, Harvard? I challenged myself with this ultimate goal. It would be extremely advantageous to study for a semester at Massachusetts General Hospital, the most famous teaching hospital in the US. But would I make it there as a German student? Although I had some doubts, I could not shake the idea, so I decided to give it a shot.

Shortly after Christmas, I took a Greyhound bus from Cleveland to Madison, Wisconsin, to start my next block of training in January 1986. Madison gets extremely cold in the winter: the houses and fields are blanketed with a thick layer of snow. Despite being the second-largest capital city in the US (after Washington, DC) and despite its many colleges, the town is actually rather provincial in character. It was here that I took up residence in a room in the home of an elderly Jewish woman, Mrs. Florence Waisman.

At the university, I was placed in Dr. Mack's group, and the daily stress began anew. For some reason I could not fathom, Dr. Mack appeared to be impressed with my work. When I told him of my hope to one day attend Harvard, he

I HAVE SEEN GOD

wasted no time in sending a detailed report about me to the medical faculty there. In his letter, he drew special attention to my desire to serve as a missionary doctor in the Third World.

With the most difficult block of study left behind in Cleveland, my working week was reduced to eighty hours. This allowed me more time to think. The "God question" resurfaced day after day. Was He really there? Or had I just been deluding myself? I did not want to just blindly believe in God – no, I actually wanted to *see* Him. One night, I lay in bed watching the ghostly shadows cast by street lights on the walls of my room. Feeling completely empty, I wept. I had prayed that God would show Himself to me – in whatever shape or form He chose. In response, there was only quiet.

At the end of February, a plane carried me to the warmth of Richmond, Virginia. The pleasant aroma of spicy tobacco pervaded the entire town. It was my first visit to the south, and the way people spoke to each other in public buildings, restaurants, and churches was both cordial and courteous. It would take little imagination to feel transported back to the time of *Gone with the Wind*.

Being the only visiting student gave me special status. As one of 3,000 students in Mainz, I had literally been just one of a crowd. But here at the Medical College of Virginia, I enjoyed special attention from students and professors alike. Douglas Palmore and his wife went out of their way to befriend me. He was the official advisor for all students, but somehow felt particularly responsible for me. When my time in Richmond came to an end, Mr. Palmore sent a glowing letter of recommendation to Harvard for me. His efforts met with success, and just a few weeks later I received a letter of acceptance into this elite university. Following my stops in Denver and Houston, my American "tour" would culminate in Boston. My acceptance was for not one but three surgery electives at Massachusetts General Hospital, MGH – or, as I learned after arrival, "Man's Greatest Hospital."

When I returned to Germany in May 1987, I had grown from an anxious student into a self-assured cosmopolitan. Over the past year and a half I had studied at six different American universities, having to prove myself over and over in constantly changing settings, and earning nine certificates of honor along the way. I knew exactly what I wanted to do: I was going to specialize as a surgeon and then make a difference in a Third-World country. Maybe I would even found my own hospital one day – why not? At the age of twenty-six, I was not lacking in self-confidence, although maybe in maturity, experience, and patience.

6

Working Until You Drop

L ife is short. I had already learned this lesson: if you wanted to achieve anything, you needed to start out strong and then pick up speed. So, just two and a half months after returning from the States, I led Tina down the aisle and we said, "I do!"

We moved into a tiny loft apartment on the west side of Wiesbaden, and began work on our doctoral theses. As a future pediatrician, Martina wrote her thesis on cystic fibrosis, a disease that typically manifests in childhood and causes progressive damage to the lungs. I conducted a pre-surgery risk assessment and analysis using a wide cross section of the patient population. We were both of the belief that investing our time and energies in scientific topics would be advantageous, and that our increased knowledge of these specialized topics would benefit our future patients much more than simply meeting the basic requirements of medical licensure.

There were moments of hardship and panic along the way. One day, I stood in the street outside Mainz University, gazing up in complete disbelief. Thick, black smoke was pouring out of the building's windows. Beyond the toxic billows was my thesis! If all my research and writing had been destroyed, I would have labored for many months in vain. The next day brought news and great relief: although the fire had caused millions of dollars' worth of damage, my study and all my hard work had been spared.

After my very positive experiences in the USA, I did not have the slightest desire to continue my career in Germany. Tina also was of the opinion that our long-term future lay in a developing country, so there was little debate. In August 1988 we packed our few belongings and moved to Great Britain to continue our training. The year in Germany had been an important transitional phase, challenging us mentally in preparation for what was to come. Besides my thesis, I had also successfully completed my German Medical Exam. Since we did not know where we would end up, Martina and I also had both taken the American Foreign Graduate Medical Exam in Frankfurt. We were young, flexible, and ready for adventure.

The British medical training program recommends that young doctors change jobs often, a concept based on the journeymen of the Middle Ages. Our two and a half years in the United Kingdom took us first to the university clinics in Cardiff and Leicester, and then on to Leeds, Bolton, and Manchester. Wherever we were, we strove to do our best. On some weekends we worked straight through from Friday morning until Monday evening without ever leaving the hospital. Tina and I had no children at this time, and we were both highly motivated and resilient. Our desire for excellent medical training was fulfilled, but not without cost. We were constantly tired and sometimes went for days without having any time together as a couple.

The British mentality agreed with us. We found the Brits to be considerably more friendly and helpful than our German countrymen. We learned a lot and could have pushed to complete our residencies in the UK, but Tina and I were up for a new challenge – this time in the USA.

Since we had passed the American Foreign Graduate Medical Exam, we had the option of transferring directly into the American system. But should we really go through such an arduous process? We prayed for weeks for God to guide us in this difficult decision. Although I still had not shaken my doubts about God, I was sincerely hoping for a nod from above.

All skepticism aside, the coming months brought so many seemingly inexplicable life events that we almost had no choice but to ascribe them to the intervention of a Higher Power.

In the summer of 1990, I sent out application packets to seventeen different US universities on the off chance that one would accept me for a residency position in the surgery department. There was no harm in knocking on the door of elite schools such as Harvard and Yale, so I applied there as well. Lo and behold, and to my great surprise, I received an offer of acceptance from Yale. Professor Cahow, Head of Surgery at the clinic in New Haven, Connecticut, was actually on sabbatical that year, but had to go into his office one day for something. My residency application was on his desk and somehow caught his eye. He opened the packet and read through my paperwork. Then he made a snap decision to bypass the admission board and offer me the position. It was probably my certificates from Harvard that clinched it.

When the news of my acceptance to Yale reached us in England, Tina began applying to teaching hospitals in the vicinity of New Haven. A few weeks later, she received a letter from Professor Kennedy, offering a residency in Hartford. But Hartford and New Haven were over 40 miles apart! How could we organize our young married life if one of us had to commute 80 miles round-trip each day?

In the spring of 1991, I traveled to Yale to meet the department heads of the medical school. Tina came with me, and contacted Professor Kennedy on arrival. Imagine our joy and disbelief when he immediately announced he was no longer at Hartford, but was now heading the pediatrics department at Bridgeport Hospital! The clinic in Bridgeport was a mere twelve miles from New Haven, and it too had the official status of a Yale teaching hospital. Without any intervention on our part, we were both able to continue our training in programs at the renowned Yale University – for two full years, as it turned out.

7

In the Empire of the Incas

The January sky was a dull shade of gray, and a cold, damp wind blew through our clothes, as if wanting to encourage our departure from England. We took with us whatever we could cram into our Talbot Horizon, and ferried one last time across the Channel from Dover to Calais. Life on an island was now a thing of the past. After unpacking in Wiesbaden, I took the rusty old vehicle to its final resting place in an auto scrapyard.

We were to resume our training in the USA that July. With just under six months to go, we thought an extensive trip to South America was both feasible and a great opportunity. So we readied our backpacks and took an Alitalia flight to Lima, the capital of Peru. Ever since childhood I had had a burning interest in the ancient Incan culture. Now we had twelve weeks free to explore their historical locales.

Our parents' enthusiasm for the trip was not quite as great as ours. A cholera epidemic there had made the headlines even in Germany. Two terrorist organizations, "Sendero Luminoso" and "Tupac Amaru," controlled large parts of the country. Tourists were strongly advised to avoid traveling through the central highlands and rainforest. The government was aggressively fighting the pervasive threat of terrorism. Over 69,000 people lost their lives in this violent struggle, as an independent investigation later ascertained. Still, the average citizen felt as much fear and dread, if not more, of the ensuing economic crisis as he did of the bombs that exploded nightly.

Alberto Fujimori, the newly elected president of Peru, had been in office for only a few months, which had been fraught with difficulty. Under his predecessor, Alan García, the rate of inflation had skyrocketed to 7,600 per cent. Long lines outside grocery stores were a stark reflection of the hardship of daily life. And there in the middle of the turmoil were the Johns, seemingly once more attracted by potentially explosive social unrest.

So as to be better prepared for our excursions through Peru, we took a crash course in Spanish. Phrases such as "¡Hola!" and "¡Hasta luego!" (English: "Hi!" and "Bye!") were soon part of our active vocabulary. Within two weeks we were feeling well prepared for further adventures. Peru was just waiting to be discovered by us!

Looping down along the south coast via Arequipa, we made it as far as Lake Titicaca, the hightest navigable inland lake in the world. After a short flight to La Paz, we took the train from Puno to Cusco. This former capital of the Incan Empire, with its churches, temples, and fortresses, is without a doubt one of the most interesting cities in South America. In a bookshop, I bought myself a copy of *The Royal Commentaries* by Garcilaso de la Vega. This son of an Incan princess and a Spanish conquistador had written down the history of the sixteenth- century Incas, and it was so riveting that it took me only a few days to read it from start to finish.

After reading it, I saw Peru with new eyes. I realized that these impoverished Quechua Indios (Indians), the legitimate descendants of the Incas, could look back on a proud history. What kind of people had they become, so melancholy and seemingly taciturn? Four hundred years of Spanish and other oppression had taken its toll, leaving its mark on their dispirited features. It was obvious to us as we traveled through Peru that this ethnic group were in dire straits. Although the Quechuas made up nearly half the nation's population, they were marginalized by society. The felt forgotten by their government miles away in Lima, and despised by the rest of the people. This racism affected their sense of self-worth immeasurably. In the large cities such as Lima and Trujillo, the Quechuas quickly learned it was better for them to abandon their heritage.

As social outcasts, they eked out a meager existence in their mud houses, which had neither power, window panes, running water, nor sewage disposal. These deplorable living conditions were a breeding ground for a wide variety of diseases of poverty, such as tuberculosis and skin infections. Up to one in every two Quechuas had worms, and the children in particular suffered from malnutrition.

As far as healthcare in the Andes was concerned, there was still a very long way to go. The people desperately needed doctors who would roll up their sleeves and take the initiative.

Yet these inhabitants, with their past and present sufferings, needed far more than pills and injections; they hungered most of all for respect and love.

If there was ever a place on earth where a missionary hospital could unfold a vision of strength and hope, it was here.

8

The Years at Yale

After our interlude in South America, we packed up our entire home in eight suitcases and flew to the US. Tina and I rented a small house by the sea in Milford, halfway between New Haven and Bridgeport. It was made of wood and rested on several pillars, the purpose of which became clear the following spring when a storm caused the water level to rise dramatically within hours. As we looked out of the living-room window, we saw our neighbor row by.

We still have fond memories of our little house by the water, and the Third-World Evenings we held there on a regular basis. Colleagues and students would come and report on their trips to Africa, Asia, and Latin America. We paid rapt attention, for one day, sooner or later, we too would be traveling to one of these lands.

Harvard and Yale are regarded as two of the leading universities in the US, with a proud tradition of excellence. Only the best applicants gain a place at these schools, and if students do not consistently produce high-quality results, they may soon find themselves tossed out on their ear. There is an iron rule of "Publish or Perish." Every resident in surgery must hold a lecture in front of all the other students and faculty. Since I had experience in Germany and England, as well as in the US, I focussed my talk on the historical roots of surgery in these three countries.

Professor Irvin Modlin offered to be my supervisor. He was a man small in stature, but a giant in intellect. His father, a Jewish scholar, had taught the Talmud in Cape Town, South Africa. He himself possessed a rare intelligence, reading up to five books each week and heading up an impressive research lab at Yale. His team of researchers produced sixty publications each year, which were almost all printed in renowned international journals. It was not long before I joined this remarkable team.

Under his supervision, the world of science opened up to me even further. I spent countless hours in the labs and wrote scientific articles for both American and European professional journals. Professor Modlin steered us towards our next stage in life. "Klaus," he would constantly appeal to my sense of conscience, "if you want to operate a lot, then you have to go to South Africa!"

The land of *the table mountains* began to call to us. Granted, there was a civil war going on at the time, but perhaps the opportunity would offer training with the right mix of theory and practical experience.

In July 1993, we stood at the South African Airways counter at J.F.K. Airport. The airline employee almost gave himself a hernia lifting our eight heavy bags onto the conveyor belt. Beforehand, we had carefully compared several airlines' prices for excess baggage. I pulled $1,000 out of my wallet and waited to hear how much I owed. The young man gave us a kind look and waved us through. "It's OK," he affirmed, and wished us a pleasant flight. Grateful, I put the bills back in my wallet.

After this encouraging encounter, we climbed aboard our plane and prepared to change continents once more.

9

Dodging Bullets

The tension in the air was almost palpable as the first free elections following the abolition of apartheid were about to be held. The black majority were unrelenting in their push for power. As civil structures increasingly fell apart, violence and crime paralyzed large areas of daily life. Those who could afford it withdrew behind barbed wire and alarm systems, allowing guard dogs to roam free in their yards. Many South Africans, both white and black, were armed – either for self-protection or for less noble purposes.

When we arrived in Johannesburg in July 1993, the country was in a state of complete breakdown. In some areas, the situation could only be described as anarchy. Every month, about a thousand cars were hijacked. If the drivers were not killed in a hail of bullets, they lived with the trauma of the experience for the rest of their lives.

Liberated at last from their white chains, the blacks began engaging in tribal warfare with each other. On March 28, 1994, 20,000 Zulus, armed to the teeth, marched into the city center to challenge Nelson Mandela's party, the African National Congress (ANC). Fifty-three people lost their lives that day.

The future was uncertain for everyone. Many whites who had contacts in Australia, Israel, Europe, or the US fled the country – an enormous loss of intellectual potential for all strata of society, as good-quality education had previously been an exclusive privilege not extended to people of color. The white population of 5 million were sharply divided in their interests. The Afrikaner people, descendants of the Boers, were deeply rooted in the soil of their country. The English-speaking population, on the other hand, felt less of a tie to South Africa, and were much more open to the option of emigration. While these two sectors of the white population had fought bitterly in the past, the black masses were now forcing them into the same corner.

So this is where we had landed – to work for two years at the legendary Baragwanath Hospital, self-proclaimed to be the largest hospital in the southern hemisphere. Its extraordinary 3,000-bed capacity gave credence to this claim. All the patients from the neighboring township of Soweto, home to over 4 million people, were treated here.

For a university clinic, it had exceptional equipment. It was very clearly a "First-World" establishment. The patients, however, who streamed through the doors in endless columns night and day, were from impoverished local communities reflecting much more of the expected "Third-World" living conditions.

In addition to the standard working week, we each had a twenty-four-hour shift every five days. In the surgery department, we were easily examining 300 patients per day. At thirty-minute intervals, groaning men with bullet and stab wounds were brought into the emergency room.

The surgical team consisted of three experienced residents, of whom I was one. One of us would operate through the night on the critically wounded. A second would also be in another operating room amputating legs, treating burns, and lancing boils of various repugnant shapes and sizes. The third colleague had the responsibility of directing a happy young group of both South African and foreign interns in their first year of training.

One of my first profoundly sobering experiences was the discovery that many black nurses did not value human life if the patient was not from the same tribe. The sight of a Zulu patient battling for his life after a bullet wound to the head did not evoke compassion, or even professionalism, from the Xhosa nurse in the emergency room. She was making private phone calls and looked up in astonishment when I lost my patience and reprimanded her strongly. In the wards crowded with sixty beds filled with suffering patients, the night nurses often congregated in the corner, leaving the patients to beg passing doctors for help.

Medically speaking, our hopes of making a quantum leap in learning were fulfilled. I operated on hundreds of patients, even cases that I would have had minimal exposure to while in Germany. Bullet wounds to the abdomen and chest soon became routine to me.

My horizons were also broadened enormously in the areas of vascular surgery, gastroenterology, and trauma surgery. I spent four months at Hillbrow Hospital in the city center, and had the opportunity to set bones of all kinds. One Friday evening a man was brought in, his arm completely smashed, a mass of bone, muscle, and tendon. My boss, a Dutchman, slapped me on the back and said, "Klaus, stabilize the forearm bone first, then you will figure out the rest!" And, with that, he left for the weekend, leaving me to get on with it. The result, however, was not bad. The man did not lose his arm.

Many of our patients were infected with the AIDS virus. Nearly one-third of the children in Tina's pediatric unit were affected, and the number of my patients with the disease continued to rise steadily. During surgery, I accidentally pricked myself with unsterile needles from time to time. I remember the fear that was such a part of my life in those days. Was I infected? Secretly, I took blood samples in the restroom and put them through the computerized lab analysis system under an assumed patient name. After the results came back negative several times, I was finally able to relax a little.

Whenever time permitted, I would bring Tina a cola at midnight. I always knew exactly where to find her. She would be scurrying around non-stop, taking care of children who would all have been on the ICU in Germany. Adrenaline kept us going through the night, but as soon as our shifts ended, we collapsed in an exhausted heap.

In the second year, we lived on a small farm in Honeydew, to the north of the city. The property was ringed by an electric fence and protected by guard dogs, as was typical. Our neighbors, a German doctor and his South African wife, Wendy, often invited us over for dinner. The conversation almost always revolved around friends or acquaintances who had been victims of an attack. In that particular year alone, three of Wendy's girlfriends had been raped and murdered. It was easy to understand why she and her husband were contemplating emigrating.

Our two years in South Africa were filled with more than work and crime, however. We had vacation opportunities to travel around the country, and quickly became enthralled by its landscape. More than once we realized that South Africa would probably be a difficult place to leave, if it were a stable country.

Like many South Africans, I developed a passion for marathon-running during this phase of my life. Each morning before going on duty, I would run three to five miles, and twice that at weekends. Long-distance running involves unwavering determination. Persevering through hardship with my eyes on a distant goal produced a great sense of internal satisfaction.

I competed in a total of three marathons while in South Africa, and was proud to be among the top 7 per cent to reach the finish line in Waterval Boven with a time of two hours and fifty-four minutes.

On September 6, 1994, our daughter, Natalie, was born, resulting in a dramatic drop in our previous willingness to take risks. Whereas before we had felt invulnerable, we now began to think more carefully about the potential consequences of our decisions. What if one or both of us became a victim of crime? The stones that were thrown regularly at our car as we drove to the hospital now seemed much more threatening. As beautiful as the wide, open country was, the time had come to leave South Africa.

In July 1995, we again returned to Germany, this time with a new baby in tow and the intention of completing our residencies in Berlin.

I HAVE SEEN GOD

10

Setting the Course

"**M**r. John, you can pursue professorship!" With these words, Professor Neuhaus of the Virchow Clinic's surgical department was offering me a job. My studies at Harvard, my residency at Yale, and my most unusual professional development on three continents seemed to predestine me for a career in academia. I could not resist the temptation, so I signed my very first German employment contract. All of a sudden, I found myself in the rigid hierarchy of Berlin University Hospital.

At 6.30 each morning, I drove from Marwitz, an idyllic town in the northern suburbs, through the congested city streets to Wedding. I was usually in a hurry, as the unrelenting German cultural ethic of punctuality was as constricting as a tight corset. The top priority of the day was getting into the meeting room before the medical director. My well-starched coat forced me to sit upright in my chair, regardless of how tired I was. The days of casual Anglo-Saxon manners were over. At a German university clinic, one spoke only when spoken to. The director, of course, always had the final word.

Having conducted over a thousand liver transplants, Professor Neuhaus had managed to become a legend in his own time. Unlike other professors, he was friendly in manner, yet he still required 100 per cent from his residents, both at the clinic during the day and at our desks in the evening.

Tina stayed at home and got us settled in our rented row house. Over time, she was able to unpack all the boxes and make friends with the neighbors. Naturally, she was the one who got to teach Natalie her first words. I was stuck on the tense treadmill of clinic life, and was conspicuous mainly by my absence. One day, when a colleague's wife brought their young son to see the clinic, he insightfully exclaimed, "OK, Mommy – so this is the house where Daddy lives!"

Whether or not one was placed on the operating schedule was a clear indicator of one's standing in the surgical department. I could not complain. Under the supervision of senior physicians, I carried out laparoscopic gall-bladder removals and was even permitted to take out cancerous stomachs for the first time. In the evenings, I would write up my research findings from South Africa and Yale, in the hope of publishing them soon in medical journals. However, I had no energy for the new study being conducted in Berlin. Fortunately, my boss graciously gave me, the world traveler, a bit of a break in this matter. Yet the demanding work continued at an unbelievable rate. The most common surgery here was not hernia repair or appendectomy, as one might think, but liver transplants. One time, I assisted in three of these marathon surgeries within twenty-four hours, and was miraculously still standing at the end.

The first year in Berlin flew by, and I registered to take my surgeon's exam. I was quite nervous, as by this point I knew the terminology better in English than in German. Still, I passed. Now I was a qualified surgeon, and I wondered what my next step should be. To pursue professorship would mean four to six years of grueling preparation. But Tina and I had always dreamed of making a difference in the lives of those in need,

I HAVE SEEN GOD

and we wanted to give this aim our very best years. I realized that although going after a professorship might indulge my own ego, it was unlikely to change the world through science or service, an ambition I had grown to accept as my "calling."

On the recommendation of my supervisor, I had contacted Dr. Eckehard Wolff, a German missionary doctor in Quito, Ecuador. Without being too specific, I asked for feedback regarding my professional future. His written reply arrived sooner than expected, and put an immediate end to my deliberations.

"We urgently need a surgeon at the Vozandes del Oriente Hospital!" I devoured every word that Dr. Wolff had written. "The hospital is situated on the edge of the Ecuadorian jungle," he continued. "You will be able to perform every operation you have ever learned!" His itemization, however, included a number of operations I had never even assisted with, let alone carried out myself. I had no experience with Caesarean sections, ectopic pregnancies, and hysterectomies. The only thing I knew about the prostate was that it was in a man's body – but removing it? I had never encountered such a thing before.

My heart was in my mouth as I considered the details of the offer. Being the only surgeon at a jungle hospital would be chronically out of my comfort zone. But, then again, wasn't this what I had actually been working towards my entire life? In February 1997, I took a week off and flew via Air France to Quito, right on the equator. I just had to have a closer look at this place on the eastern slopes of the Andes.

Dr. Wolff and his wife, Klaudia, also a missionary doctor, picked me up from the airport themselves and got me settled in their own home. Their hospitality knew no bounds. Perhaps they thought that with five children of their own, another two or three at the table would not make any great difference. Two days later, a small Cessna belonging to Mission Aviation Fellowship took me over the Andes to my destination of Shell. The oil company of the same name had reportedly drilled at this site fifty years ago in search for the "black gold," but to no avail. The drilling rigs had long since been removed, and all that remained of that failed endeavor was the handed-down name and the small runway on which our single-engine aircraft now came to a bumpy halt. As the door opened, I was assaulted by the extreme heat and humidity of the rainforest. As I would soon discover, the high humidity vented itself nearly every half hour in a tropical downpour.

Dr. Roger Smalligan, an American missionary doctor, showed me every nook and cranny of the hospital, which had been founded by American missionaries in 1958. He was obviously doing all he could to promote the appeal of working here, as the hospital had not had a permanent surgeon under contract in about six years. Visiting surgeons from all over the world helped out sporadically; hence the number of scheduled operations was subject to the fluctuating availability of qualified staff. At this point, there was *one* surgical patient in the ward. I struggled to hide my disappointment, as I had been anticipating the pulsating activity of a South African hospital. The only noise here was caused by the tropical storms bringing torrential rain that pounded against roofs and windows like bursts of machine-gun fire. Was this tiny clinic with its twenty-five beds where I was meant to be? I was filled with uncertainty. The hospital made a rather "backwoods" impression, and had certainly seen better days.

The week in Ecuador went by in a flash. I had no idea whether or not I would ever return to this isolated place. As I waited at Quito Airport for my return flight to Germany,

I was not in a good frame of mind. The flight was delayed and this did nothing to improve my mood. A flight attendant came into the departure area and spoke to a few passengers, including a rather corpulent man I had down as a German tourist. When the young woman left, I immediately went up to him and asked if he knew what was causing the delay. He had no idea either, and the conversation ended as abruptly as it had begun.

At long last our flight was called, and we boarded the plane that would take us over the clouds to the Colombian capital of Bogotá. Here we had a long layover, as our scheduled connection to Paris was not due for another two hours. We were herded into a massive transit hall where we could sit or even lie down anywhere we chose, as there were rows and rows of empty chairs. I sat down in bored isolation and pulled out a book of short stories.

"So, we meet again!" A heavy body dropped into the seat next to me, and I recognized the big man from Quito.

"What a nerve!" I thought to myself. "With hundreds of empty seats, you should respect people's right to a little privacy and hang out elsewhere!" Attempting to discourage further dialogue, I murmured a few incomprehensible words and indicated the book I was attempting to read.

"So what brought you to Ecuador?" The man pulled his chair closer. It looked as if I had been chosen to help him pass the time until our flight. My answers were very short, almost rude, as I was still hoping he would pick up the hint that I had no desire to engage in some affable conversation. I moved the book closer to my face. Surely, if this man had any clue about body language, he would get the message and go away.

He didn't.

I sighed with the bitter realization that the man was just

not going to leave me alone. I snapped my book shut, and turned to give Mr. Nosy the information he was asking for. I told him of my visit to the Vozandes del Oriente Hospital and Martina's and my possible plan to serve long-term in Ecuador as missionary doctors.

"Are you a member of a particular church?" he asked. My plans probably seemed a little weird to my tireless interrogator, and he must have come to the conclusion that I was an odd duck, maybe even a religious nut.

"I attend a small church of a denomination you are probably not familiar with."

That didn't satisfy him. "So what is it called?"

"It's an Evangelical Free church."

"You don't say!" His amazed expression suddenly turned into intense interest in the dialogue that had been bubbling along for a while now. "I belong to an Evangelical Free church is Essen!" There was a short break as we both processed this unexpected turn in the conversation. "And I lead our church's outreach program to developing nations. Maybe we could support your work in Ecuador!"

My unexpected meeting with a man I had not particularly liked at first sight grew more and more intriguing.

"My name is Wolfgang Hasselhuhn." Bearing in mind how long we had already been talking, it was high time we introduced ourselves. Then he took a deep breath and started sharing some personal details that would have touched even the most callous of hearts.

"My wife died of lung cancer four weeks ago." He spoke slowly, and every word weighed heavily on him. "I was in a deep, dark hole," he continued. "And then my brother invited me to stay with him. He has been serving as an aid worker in Ecuador for several years now. He thought it was time for me to get out and see something different!" Mr. Hasselhuhn and I looked each other in the eye. Deep inside, we felt a bond between us.

This was the moment I felt the "nod from above" I had so long been praying for. The question that had been nagging at me all week had just been answered. My wife and I would go to Ecuador as missionary doctors, and Mr. Hasselhuhn, whom I hadn't even known a few minutes ago, would work with his church in Essen to raise part of our support. I felt like a child who has just received the best Christmas gift ever!

Wolfgang too stepped out of the transit hall and boarded the plane to Paris as a winner. One month after losing his wife, he now felt renewed purpose in his life and had a meaningful task to fulfill. He did indeed make a significant contribution towards enabling Tina and me to serve as missionary doctors. Seventeen years have passed since this mysterious encounter in Bogotá.

Wolfgang Hasselhuhn managed to elicit the support of his missions committee and eventually the whole church. They remain among our most loyal supporters. I would estimate that they themselves have raised around €20,000 (approximately $30,000) for us and our projects. When we were on the edge of our biggest project yet – the building of a modern hospital in Peru – the ripple effect from the work of this one church resulted in an additional €100,000 (approximately $150,000) worth of donations for hospital equipment.

Neither Wolfgang nor I doubt that God arranged for our paths to cross in Quito and then again in Bogotá.

When I returned to duty at the surgical clinic, I was bursting with enthusiasm as I shared our plans to move to Ecuador. My colleagues shook their heads in disbelief. I sensed an undercurrent of pity in their tone, and learned that my answered prayer was commonly regarded as a "naïve impulse." Instead of pursuing a professorship, popular opinion was that I would "vegetate" in some jungle hospital and thoroughly ruin my career in the process.

Professor Neuhaus also heard of our plans. His reaction was swift and retaliatory. I was put on ICU duty as a "disciplinary measure," and I was not permitted to operate for the remainder of my contract. The professorship he encouraged had been an offer. I had turned it down, and now there was a price to pay. But I did not lose courage. After the meeting with Wolfgang Hasselhuhn, I was absolutely sure I was doing the right thing.

In the summer of 1997, my contract with the university was up, and Tina went back to work to complete her residency in pediatrics. I stayed home for the year and took care of the children, for we now had two: Dominik had come along in 1996. I spent the daytime with the children, but in the evening, after they had gone to bed, I worked feverishly at my desk, preparing for our departure for Ecuador. Soon we would be officially considered "missionary doctors," although perhaps some clarification is needed here. Tina and I had always openly said that we wanted to serve as doctors in a Third-World country and that we were Christians. "Christian" of course relates to Christ, and I was very familiar with His teachings. At this point, I had almost completely overcome my previous doubts about God. His power was once again real to me, just as it had been many years before when I had left to study in the States. My own mysterious experiences and answers to prayer did not allow for any other conclusion. I did not, however, feel called or motivated to impose my private faith on others.

I held a total of fifty presentations in churches, clubs, and hospitals, sharing the dream of our future mission in the Andes. Tina came with me when she could. We printed literally thousands of flyers describing our plans and asking for support. Anybody who was interested could send in the reply card indicating their desired pledge for monthly support. The VDM missionary society in Bassum, Germany took us under contract on the condition that we raise our own financial support. This means that a lot of generous people agreed to finance us long-term, paying not only the employer's share but also our share of the taxes and cost of government benefits typically deducted from one's salary. In addition to earning enough to live on, Tina and I wanted to pay into a medical pension plan. After consulting with other missionary doctors, we set a goal of raising $5,000 per month. After all deductions, we would be making about $1,500 each for working full-time as a surgeon and a pediatrician respectively.

A day before we left for Ecuador, I hit the RETURN key on my computer, and in a fraction of a second the EXCEL program calculated the total of support pledged by the 100 people turning in the reply cards. I could scarcely believe my eyes: the bottom line was $5,000. After a year of public relations work, friends and relatives had pledged the exact sum of money we had been aiming for. Not one dollar more or less.

11

Under the Equatorial Sun

On a radiant September morning, the KLM plane descended for landing at Quito Airport. The runway was set like a rectangle in the middle of the city. The altitude of 7,500 feet and situation in the mountains made this a challenge for even the most skilled pilots. As our Boeing 737 throttled back, it rolled past a burned-out Russian Tupolev, which, just three weeks earlier, had crashed into the fence at the end of the runway and gone up in flames.

Before us, the eternal ice of Mt. Cotopaxi was resplendent in the glistening rays of the rising sun. At 19,000 feet, the cone-shaped volcano sat enthroned majestically, if somewhat threateningly, on the horizon. In the course of past centuries, its eruptions had razed the base city of Latacunga to the ground four times. But today, in place of molten lava, it cast only reflections of light to welcome us from seventy miles away.

We were inundated with thousands of new experiences: this was truly an adventure unlike any other. This time it was not me making a visit with my backpack. This time we were a family of four getting started on a whole new life in a different culture with an unfamiliar language. We rented a house belonging to missionaries who were home on furlough in the US.

Within days, we began learning Spanish. A friendly Ecuadorian woman came to our house every day for two

61

I HAVE SEEN GOD

hours and practiced the first halting conversations with Tina and me. Natalie (four) and Dominik (two) went through a similar culture shock as they attended a nearby preschool for two or three hours each day. Although they would chatter freely at home, it was months before they spoke a word to the local Ecuadorian children.

"Hey, Klaus, coming with us?" Friedemann Becker asked in a way that presumed an affirmative response. "Pastor Rolando and I are visiting a Quechua village in the south."

The offer was enticing. To live with the Indios for three days was surely the best way to really get to know them and become familiar with their way of life. It was November and the rainy season had not yet started. I was in.

For hours on end, the bus toiled over the western mountain chain of the Andes. I sat next to Friedemann Becker, who had been serving for the last eight years as a missionary pastor to the Quechua Indios of Ecuador. Behind me, Señor Rolando Martinez dozed in his seat, his head lolling from side to side as we rounded the sharp bends. Ten years earlier, he had been spreading fear and dread throughout Peru as one of the leading members of the well-known "Sendero Luminoso" terrorist group. Now, as a pastor, he was telling the Quechuas of Ecuador why he had renounced his previous life of violence. His faith in Christ had changed him completely.

Our destination was the Quechua village of Cascajal in the foothills of the Andes. Arriving in the evening, we were immediately welcomed into the community. Over 200 Indios had gathered in a forest clearing, which was dimly illuminated by a few lamps. At around 8 p.m., a band started the musical part of the program. The songs sung in Quechua and Spanish, accompanied by drums and electric guitar, rang through the air with such volume and energy that they resonated even in the neighboring settlement. The preaching began three hours later, and the service ended in prayer at midnight. Moved, I returned to our quarters, a wooden hut on the brink of a deep gorge, and crept into my sleeping bag. Had I ever experienced such passionate devotion as I had just witnessed among these Indios?

The next morning began with a march down to the river. The water was ice cold, but... the things one must do to stay clean. For breakfast, there was warm soup, a dish of rice, and some meat. A couple of dozen Indios sat in a circle with us and seemed to enjoy seeing us accept their hospitality. I took advantage of my time there by asking many questions: "Where is the nearest hospital?" "Where do you go when you are sick?" The picture I was presented with was truly appalling. Medical care for the half a million Quechuas in the province of Chimborazo (just like everywhere else in the Andes) was horrible beyond description. Travel to one of the distant towns with better medical facilities was unaffordable for most of them. Sickness and death loomed over the Quechuas like a dense, inescapable fog of fate.

The last evening, or rather, *night*, the service had finished and at 1 a.m. we were standing waiting for the bus. A group of Indios waited with us, serving us rice and fish to strengthen us for the journey home. As we struggled to eat the generous portions, the leader of the congregation thrust the bus fare in our jacket pockets, nodding his head in gratitude. I looked down at my plate, ashamed. How could I take money from a man who really had none to spare and lived with only the most basic necessities?

At last, the headlights of the bus shone through the dark. As we slowly climbed aboard, twenty or thirty hands stretched through the door towards us. Small children, old men, and young women demonstrated their love for us one last time. In the few remaining seconds, I shook as many hands as I possibly could.

The bus snorted and sputtered up the steep curves of the mountains. The hum of the engine was incredibly soothing, and within three minutes I had fallen asleep, overcome by exhaustion.

Many years later, I could still see those outstretched hands and hear the words of gratitude. My decision the year before to serve as a missionary doctor for the Indios had been a pure "head" decision, in the sense of basic right and wrong. The visit to Cascajal had involved my heart in the matter as well. I wanted to build these people a hospital one day. The hands stretched through the door had not been begging for anything, but I sensed in their manner an unvoiced cry for help. I would not ignore it, for, odd and unexpected as it seemed, I had come to love these mountain Indios.

We celebrated our first Christmas in South America with many other missionaries. We were still learning the language and battling bravely to broaden our Spanish vocabulary. But, at that party, almost everyone seemed to be speaking English, so we happily joined in.

I was particularly excited by talking to a rather stocky American who introduced himself as John Walter. I had heard rumors that he was a civil engineer and knew a great deal about building hospitals. "What do you think?" I asked him. "How much would it cost to build a new mission hospital here in South America?"

If Mr. Walter thought my question odd, or maybe even insane, his face did not show it. "There's a formula for calculating that," he said, "based on the number of square feet!"

Seven years later, the construction vehicles were to roll

in 1,500 miles away in neighboring Peru. Heading up the construction crew was none other than John Walter.

In February 1999 we traveled to Shell, where our future workplace, the Vozandes del Oriente Hospital, was located. In the pouring rain, we drove through town at a snail's pace, trying to find somewhere to live. Through the steamed-up windows, we made out the shape of an appealing little house with a covered porch. We stopped and knocked on the door. An Ecuadorian military officer of about thirty years of age opened the door.

"Would you consider renting us this house?" The question did not seem to surprise him. He discussed the matter briefly with his wife, and we immediately began negotiating the details of a rental contract.

Like most buildings in the area, the house was not completely finished. We agreed on a substantial down payment so that in the next six weeks up to our official move-in date, all necessary structural changes could be taken care of. First of all, the house needed a wall for protection against intruders, an entrance gate, and bars on the windows. The interior needed some redecorating as well. "Don't worry!" our new landlord promised. "It will all be done to your utmost satisfaction!"

In Quito, we had bought some furniture, and so we came back in early May with a small truckfull. As we rounded the corner and wheezed to a stop outside our little rented house, our mouths fell open in shock and dismay. No wall, no gate, no bars at the windows. Inside, a few Ecuadorians were casually slapping paint on the walls with brushes. We could not believe what we were seeing. It was a while before we learned that arrangements and promises regarding time were not taken that seriously in Latin America. They are regarded as statements of intent, but everyone pretty much knows and accepts that actual practice is quite different. Things get done when they get done: simple as that.

On May 10, 1999, I started work at the legendary Vozandes del Oriente Hospital. I had not stepped into an operating room in three years, and I was feeling more than a little apprehensive. But there was no time to ease into the new job. In Puyo, capital of the Pastaza Province, the annual city carnival was taking place. In the midst of the festivities, a young motorbike rider apparently had a sudden urge to turn round and kiss his girlfriend, who was riding behind him on the bike. This amorous gesture resulted in disaster as the bike careened into an oncoming truck. Both the young man and his girlfriend had serious multiple fractures and needed to get to a hospital immediately. But which hospital? Owing to the carnival, the doctors at the three nearest hospitals were unavailable. And so a motor convoy brought the pair to Shell, where I first stabilized the fractures at midnight. A few days later, the young couple were airlifted to Quito for further treatment.

Two weeks later, Dr. Michael Stathis arrived from Australia. This veteran surgeon had agreed to work alongside me for two months to make the transition easier: a very welcome offer. We spent a very pleasant time together and I learned a great deal from him. One Tuesday morning, we were just removing a thyroid gland when Steve Manock, one of the general practitioners, burst into the operating room. He was extremely agitated. "You have to do an emergency C-section – otherwise the child will die!"

We had only one anesthesiologist, and we were the only surgeons – surgeons who happened already to be right in the middle of a tricky procedure. "Steven, send the woman to Puyo. This operation is going to take at least another hour," I murmured from behind my protective mask.

But Dr. Manock persisted. "Either we deliver the child by C-section *now* or it will be too late!"

Within seconds we had a crisis plan. I ran into the neighboring operating room with a medical student, and prepared mentally for my first ever C-section. The anesthesiologist followed me and started the machine for the anesthetic. After a two-minute introduction to the art of anesthesia, Steve Manock took over the machine in the first operation room.

My pulse was certainly racing faster than the baby's heartbeat at this point. After a quick prayer, I found my way through the abdominal wall and within no time was holding the newborn in my hands. The baby gave a loud cry, and air rushed in to fill the lungs. I too breathed a sigh of relief.

In the course of my four and a half years at the mission hospital, I was to carry out 2,000 operations that were as varied as the conditions that necessitated them. I was very familiar with general surgery after my seven years' residency. Operations on gall bladders, appendixes, colons, hernias, and amputations were all part of my original training, and I felt secure in these skills. This was not the case initially with hysterectomies, ectopic pregnancies, ovarian cysts, and C-sections. But I learned to do all of these, as well as prostate surgery from the specialty of urology. With fractures and tendon injuries, I always consulted my small library of textbooks.

From day one, I kept written records of my patients and conscientiously, if somewhat reluctantly, noted any complications that ensued. I never began an operation without asking for God's protection. Of my first 1,000 patients, not one of them died owing to complications during surgery. Today, I can only ascribe this miraculous outcome to the blessing of God.

Many of the endless hours in the operating room are indelibly etched on my memory. The sometimes desperate struggle to save the life of a patient who had been brought into hospital in a state of shock stayed with me well into the night. Unlike in the large clinics in Europe and the US, missionary doctors in developing nations often work in near isolation. There is no one there to provide competent assistance. Being thrown into these life-and-death battles requires one's learning curve to become nearly vertical. I gained a great deal of skill and experience, as well as a fair amount of gray hair.

Some stories read like thrillers. Such was the case when the phone rang and a doctor on the northern edge of the rainforest informed us, "We have a young man here who jumped into the river this morning and impaled himself on a post!" His tone of voice told me that the young man was fighting for his life. The doctor continued gravely, "The wood has penetrated the chest wall into the lung, then through the diaphragm into the liver. Can you help?"

He had already attempted to have the seriously injured patient airlifted to Quito. But just the day before, the Pichincha volcano at the city gates had erupted for the first time in a hundred years. The runway was covered with ash and the airport subsequently had to be closed. With no feasible alternative, we agreed to take the patient.

The next morning, a Cessna flew the half-dead young Shuar Indio to Shell. The ambulance was ready and waiting, as was the surgical team. I opened his chest and abdominal cavities and found a sea of blood. The recovery period took months, but he survived!

Mission hospitals are usually characterized by highly motivated staff. The missionaries from Europe and the US do not do their jobs for money; healing the sick is an outward expression of their faith. This is why they jump out of bed in the middle of the night without complaining. If there is a need, they are there – an attitude seldom found in Third-World state hospitals.

I always had five consecutive weeks of on-call duty, night and day. The phone was right by my pillow, ready for me to grab. If it rang at night, I could jump right into my shoes. And that is exactly what happened early one Sunday morning. At 5 a.m. it was still dark outside, and everyone was still snuggled up, fast asleep. In the midst of this pre-dawn tranquility, an ambulance screeched to a halt in front of the hospital. Two Ecuadorian doctors were holding towels against a man's neck, trying to stem profuse bleeding. During a knife fight, the blade had sliced right through to the base of this Indio's skull, severing the major vein in his neck.

For some inexplicable reason, no surgeons were available in Puyo that night. As I ran to the hospital, other missionaries were dragged out of bed to donate blood. Within minutes, five of them were holding out their arms to give their blood to save this stranger's life. The first donor was Dr. Roger Smalligan, general practitioner and medical director of the clinic.

No sooner had several ounces of blood been drawn from him than Dr. Smalligan hurried to the operating room to assist me. I could see and tie off the bottom part of the vein in the depths of the wound, but I simply could not get at the base of the skull, no matter how deep we went. Still, somehow, I managed to plug the wound and stop the bleeding.

The surgical team took a break to discuss the next course of action. Fearing new bleeding, I was in favor of transporting the patient to the hospital in Quito. Dr. Smalligan immediately got on the phone to the largest state hospital, located in the capital. The Eugenio Espejo Hospital was open to poor patients, although its standard of care was much lower than would be found in the private clinics that served the affluent upper class.

The news from Quito was quite sobering. "But it's carnival time," the nurse said. "There will be no surgeons at the hospital for the next three days!"

And so we kept the patient with us until he eventually could be released a few days later.

Missionary doctors usually work in poorly resourced facilities with obsolete equipment. Broken machines and chronic shortages of both money and staff make it necessary to improvise almost constantly. This lack of security often causes doctors and nurses to seek refuge in prayer. I was no exception.

I clearly remember a case of an abdominal hernia. The sac was indeed impressive. I carefully moved through the layers of tissue and tried to get a general idea of the scope, but the longer I fiddled with scissors and knife, the less clear things became, until two hours later I no longer knew which way was up. Discouraged, I put down the instruments. The anesthesiologist, Dr. Kime, a retiree from the US, saw my plight. Together we stood in the corner of the operating room and prayed out loud for God to help us. Ten minutes later, I knew exactly what I had to do, and the surgery was completed successfully within a short time.

A similar thing happened with a gallstone trapped in the lower bile duct. The poor patient had survived an eight-hour journey on a gravel road in the hope that we could relieve her suffering. It was no trouble to cut away the gall bladder, but the stone would not budge, no matter what tricks we tried. Hours went by and I finally gave up.

At that moment, Dr. Kime prayed, "God, You said that if

70

we had faith the size of a mustard seed, we would be able to move mountains. This is just a tiny stone. Please help us." I fed the tube into the duct one last time. Seconds later, the stone slid into the duodenum and we were home.

Praying before and during surgery is the only key to success for me. I can only confirm that the more you trust God and realize your dependence on Him, the more help you will see from above.

Following one of my presentations at a Rotary Club meeting in Wolfenbüttel, a retired senior surgeon came up to me to express his appreciation. "The best part," he said as he shook my hand vigorously, "was that you always pray in the operating room. I used to do that in my day too, albeit quietly."

Each evening at 9 p.m., I did the rounds on the ward to check on my patients. Monitoring them so closely contributed significantly to their recovery. I was enjoying my work more and more, but deep inside I knew that our years at Shell were just the preparation for something else, something *big*. Tina and I had talked repeatedly about building our own mission hospital for the poor. We had noticed that over the course of our time here, more of the poor patients seemed to be turned away. The hospital simply didn't have the funds, and so there was a clear shift towards a more financially solvent, middle-class clientele. But we had not given up our careers to serve the rich. Our desire to build a new missionary hospital in the Andes, one specifically for the poor, grew more and more pressing. It was time to act.

Dreaming of a hospital is one thing; actually planning one is completely different. One dismal September evening, I was sitting in a guest house in Quito, staring at the white wall. My thoughts troubled me. How were my wife and I ever going to manage to get such a massive project started? Were we deluding ourselves? Was this a pipe dream that could never really materialize? I knew the odds against our success were seemingly insurmountable.

Despondently, I opened my small devotional journal at the page for that day and read Psalm 32. When I got to the eighth verse, the words almost literally jumped off the page at me and my dark mood evaporated completely, for I read: "God says: I will instruct you and teach you in the way you should go; I will counsel you and watch over you."

My brain kicked into high gear. If God could instruct me step by step and give me all the right contacts, then everything would indeed be possible! My realization of this powerful promise gave way to euphoria. I suddenly had the rock-solid conviction that this mission hospital not only could be built, but *would* be built. It was not I who would bear financial responsibility for it, but God. He would take me by the hand and let me know what action I needed to take and when.

Every great vision is born at a definite moment in time. For Diospi Suyana, it was September 27, 2000. Since that day, I have never doubted that the project would be carried through to completion. Of course, I had no idea that I would one day travel 200,000 miles around Europe and the US to take the vision of Diospi Suyana into churches, clubs, and homes. But the inner assurance that would sustain me even through the difficult "desert" times was born in that one pivotal moment.

12

The Starting Signal

So Martina and I were to found a hospital. To be more accurate, it would not actually be us founding it, but rather God through us. But I had no knowledge or experience of project development in general, or of planning hospitals in particular. I realized I would need to do research and ask lots of questions, preferably of people who could give me solid answers.

On October 2, 2000, I traveled to Peru and Bolivia for a second time. On the recommendation of a Peruvian acquaintance, I went first to a small Christian medical station in Chilimarca, near Cochabamba, Bolivia. A Columbian doctor by the name of José Miguel de Angulo headed up the clinic.

When I told him of my long-term plan to build a mission hospital, he was bluntly critical. I had not found an advocate in him. However, before sending me on my way, he did sell me a copy of *A New Agenda for Medical Missions*, a book that proved to be a valuable source of both information and perspective to me a year and a half later. For example, it placed emphasis not on building hospitals in isolation, but on simultaneously developing local healthcare systems.

A few days later, I flew in a small plane from La Paz over Lake Titicaca to Cusco to meet the English missionary doctor,

73

Nat Davis. In the 1970s, he had worked in a mission hospital in Urcos, an hour's drive south of Cusco. He did not think my plans were crazy fantasies; he took me quite seriously. As he was to tell me years later, he was convinced upon our meeting that this hospital would one day be built. The "where" and "when" were not yet clear, but, for him, there was no longer a question of "if" or "whether."

In January 2001, I returned to Peru for a third time, now accompanied by my wife and children. Joined by Nat Davis, we examined the remains of the old clinic in Urcos. There was no trace of its once great past. Its broken windows and crumbling plaster seemed to cry out for the demolition company to come, as they were sure no new clinic would ever rise from these ruins like a phoenix from the ashes.

In the afternoon, we sat in the Davis family's living room and talked about the new hospital as though millions of dollars were just sitting ready in an account for our use, and bodies of experts had already drawn up detailed plans for the hospital's development. An outsider would have found the scene completely ridiculous.

"It may interest you to know," Dr. Davis said with a smile, "that this morning, members of my church called to ask exactly when the hospital would be opening…"

That's what faith can do.

Like good tourists, we took the children on the train up to Machu Picchu, where we were all enthralled by the magic of that mystical Incan city. What a thought – to be able to live and work nearby!

For one long year, nothing at all happened that would suggest progress towards our vision. On the other hand, we had more than enough to keep us busy at the Vozandes del Oriente Hospital. Things were stirring deep within us, but we simply did not know how to take the first step forward.

On January 18, 2002, I was standing in our bedroom, phone in hand, asking co-worker Steve Manock for travel tips for a more local trip we wanted to take. It was the weekend, and, for a change, I wasn't working.

"Oh, by the way," Steve said, suddenly changing the subject, "our colleague Jane Weaver is having difficulty getting her permit to serve as a missionary doctor in Quito. What do you think about having her come to Shell for a year?"

I rejected this idea immediately. Jane was a young American surgeon, and if she came to us, the number of my operations would be cut from 600 to 300 per year. I was just about to make a sharp protest to Steve when Tina intervened. "Klaus," she whispered, "we want to build a hospital. You will need time. Let Jane come!"

I looked at Tina, dumbfounded. What she had said had suddenly rocked me out of the rut that had been impeding our progress. Something caused me to listen to her.

"Steve, yes, sure, I have no problem with Jane coming. She can operate as much as she wants."

I carefully replaced the receiver and looked across at Tina. With sudden determination, she spoke softly but assertively: "We are both over forty. Either we tackle the project now or it will be too late!"

It is difficult to put into words, but we both sensed that the starting signal had just been given for our long-cherished dream.

The next morning, I sat down at my desk and wrote the first page of a project draft. Three and a half years later, it was to lead to the ground-breaking ceremony for the hospital in Curahuasi, Peru. In retrospect, the original wording of the first two paragraphs proved almost prophetic. The text breathed certainty over a miracle no one in Peru, Ecuador, or Germany could ever have envisioned. No one except us.

> *The present draft describes the development of a mission hospital for the Indios of Peru or Bolivia. It states the reasons in favor of such a construction and outlines the possible steps towards the completion of this project, to be further determined via the implementation of a feasibility study. The idea for this work has emerged over the years in the minds of my wife, Martina, and myself.*

A little further down, I wrote:

> *A project such as a medical clinic cannot be devised from scratch overnight. We are aware that the planning and preliminary work may stretch over years. Many people will be alongside to advise and inspire so that the final product will be a team result.*
>
> *In all our planning, it is our utmost desire to seek God's blessing and guidance in prayer.*

For six long months, I made use of every free minute in the evenings and at weekends to read up on necessary subjects. I bought books about Peru and Bolivia, and underlined relevant points in pencil. I carefully studied maps of both countries, and probed anybody I met who knew more about South America than I did.

When I found the old floorplan of the Shell hospital in a dusty corner, I copied the draft conscientiously onto my computer. I then considered what improvements could be made to the existing building. By identifying and analyzing the shortcomings here, I intended to avoid replicating them in the new hospital. In my mind, I could visualize a modern hospital with its own ICU, endoscopy and dental areas, a generous auditorium, a shop, and adequate storage. Of course, it would also have multiple operating rooms, X-ray facilities, and private rooms for consulting with patients. By June, the initial draft was complete. Over the span of fifty pages, it provided a detailed rationale for the construction of such a hospital. It also outlined possible locations, the objective of our work, financial and management details, and our plan for creating support organizations in both Germany and South America.

For good measure, I included a sketch of the hospital as I could visualize it. I described the individual stages of building with a precise schedule from inception through to completion. The whole thing would, without a doubt, be expensive. We estimated 2 to 3 million dollars for construction and equipment. We would also need between twenty-five and thirty volunteers realistically to implement the plan.

Tina read each page carefully and made her own additions. In the summer of 2002, we made twenty copies of the proposal and sent them to friends and acquaintances, boldly asking them if they would be willing to join us in setting up a support organization. Ironically, Jane Weaver stayed in Quito, and I continued to perform fifty operations each month. It was pure enthusiasm and inspiration that kept me awake each evening in the light of my desk lamp.

13

Ten People Decide to Take Action

"The Johns are losing touch with reality!" Many of our acquaintances who had generously and faithfully supported our work in Ecuador for years were becoming concerned. We understood where they were coming from. Planning to build a large hospital in a South American country 6,500 miles from home was enough to raise more than a few eyebrows. Knowing we had neither financial capital nor viable connections in the country itself did not exactly inspire confidence either.

When Tina and I traveled back to Germany in July 2002, we were seeking people to stand with us and to set up an official support organization. Of course, we had never done anything like this before, but according to our schedule, this was the next thing that needed to happen. We sought advice and learned that, according to German law, a minimum of seven members would need to be present at the constituting sessions. We had indeed sent our project proposal to potential supporters, but who would actually commit to getting mixed up in such a dubious venture?

My sister Helga could not imagine that people in Germany would be willing to bear any personal responsibility for a risky undertaking like this. Good friends in Berlin showed interest, but suggested trimming the scale down to just a small medical station, a more "realistic" endeavor. Another advisor inquired how we would pay back our financial supporters if the plan flopped after six months. Tina and I really had not factored in this type of contingency.

Our enthusiasm was apparently less than contagious. Concern that we had got carried away with this "obsession," particularly in such economically challenging times, was no doubt well-meaning. Our parents and in-laws shook their heads. How were the millions we had so casually put in our proposal ever going to materialize? Not to mention the long-term running costs?

As Tina and I wanted to be in South America to build and manage the hospital, we needed someone energetic to help with the organizational development in Germany. Olaf Böttger came to mind, one of the young men in my youth group during the 1970s. He had always been a man of integrity, both conscientious and competent. Many years had passed, but I was able to track down his number and give him a call.

"Olaf, we need a suitable chairperson for our organization in Germany," I said outright. "Isn't that your thing?"

Olaf was not the type to rush into a commitment he could not see through. So he asked a few questions about how much time and responsibility might be involved. I honestly could not give him an exact answer. "Oh, you know, once you get going, things get so much easier," I replied vaguely, attempting to allay his concerns. Naturally, Olaf would need to discuss such a weighty decision with his wife, Kathrin.

On August 17, 2002, it was not just the requisite seven but ten people who met in Tabarz, Thuringia. In addition to Tina and myself, there were another eight who had traveled from the Rhein-Main area and Berlin. Gisela Graf from Wiesbaden was one of them. Her husband, Ulrich, had actually only wanted to accompany her to the meeting venue, but he found the atmosphere so friendly and cordial that he decided on the spot to become a founding member too. The hotel was not far from Wartburg, where Martin Luther had translated the New Testament into German centuries earlier. Why shouldn't a positive force go out from this part of Germany a second time? When Olaf Böttger announced after careful consideration that he was in fact willing to assume the responsibility of chairing the organization, it was a great relief. We knew he was absolutely the right man for the job in Germany.

For two full days, we composed and honed the statutes. We chose the expression "Diospi Yuyana" as a temporary name. This suggestion, from Dr. Nat Davis, meant something akin to "We trust in God." This was not only the name but also the testimony, as, apart from God, we humbly acknowledged we could do nothing. On the recommendation of linguists, we changed the name the following year to "Diospi Suyana."

As we posed for a group photo, we could clearly imagine the mission hospital far away, where mountain Indios would be treated with love and respect. But whether this vision would become reality in three, five, or ten years, we could not know – much as we would have liked to.

14

Peru or Bolivia?

In October, Tina and I sent a newsletter to over 500 friends in sixteen different countries. It contained a subtle intimation that we as a family were looking forward to a new horizon. Where exactly that horizon might be was not at all clear. Owing to their comparable social structure, both Peru and Bolivia were possibilities. It was no good debating from afar; I needed to go myself and search in both countries for the location God had planned for us.

I had planned a three-week "expedition" in January–February 2003. I was dreading it – traveling from one town to the next in overcrowded, rickety old buses, arriving exhausted at seedy hotels. The prospect did nothing to awaken the "wanderlust" in me. The most critical task I needed to accomplish was meeting with competent representatives of the state, of local churches, and of health departments. There was absolutely no point to standing in random market squares, announcing the construction of a new mission hospital like some biblical prophet.

The trip, as necessary as it was, weighed heavily on me. A deep sense of disquiet drove me to prayer. In that crucial experience back in September 2000, God had promised to instruct me in the way I should go. At least that was how I had interpreted that moment of enlightenment in Quito. Now it was time to claim that promise.

Before starting at Vozandes del Oriente, I often used to meet up with Dr. Brad Quist. He shared my love of distance running, and as we always started our course slowly, there was a chance to talk.

"Klaus, you should talk to Apollo Landa!"

"Who is that?" I asked.

"A Peruvian doctor who works for a Christian organization in South America. His office is in Quito."

A few weeks later, Tina and I knocked on Dr. Landa's door. South Americans tend to exchange pleasantries for half an hour before getting to the point of a meeting. But not us. We had stated our purpose in coming before we had even reached the living room. We were just sitting down on the couch when Dr. Landa called out to his wife in the kitchen, "The province of Abancay would be the right area for a hospital, don't you think, Pilar?"

He had no way of knowing that I had already come to exactly that conclusion after studying the map. Abancay incorporated a major junction of two important Peruvian roads, and was an area of extreme poverty.

Apollo Landa was well connected and promised to mobilize his network on our behalf. Among other things, he was able to arrange a meeting for me with the Director of the Council of Evangelical Churches in both La Paz and Lima.

Access to the government in both countries came about in equally surprising ways. Horst Rosiak, a missionary from the German-language section of the HCJB radio station in Quito, urged me to visit Dr. Martin Ruppenthal, who, as Director of the Christoffel Mission for the Blind, was responsible for 120 related projects in South America. Following his advice,

82

I called Dr. Ruppenthal and requested an appointment that same week. Lo and behold, my little laptop presentation did in fact move Dr. Ruppenthal to offer me an audience with the Ministers of Health in both capital cities. I had no idea how he was going to pull this off, but I was open to a pleasant surprise.

In October, Markus Rolli arrived unexpectedly in Shell. He had traveled all the way from Switzerland to work at the mission hospital for three months. Markus is an all-round talent. When he heard of my travel plans, he offered to come with me – at his own expense. I felt immense relief. The long trips through unknown territory were not only safer but also less lonely for two traveling together.

Before we embarked on our journey, a small matter needed to be addressed. Since we would be meeting people of influence, our attire needed to be slightly more upscale. Markus had brought only comfortable, practical clothing for travel. He tried on my blue suit in our living room, and something happened that I have absolutely no explanation for. Although Markus is four inches taller than me, and thin as a rake, my suit looked as if it had been tailor-made for him.

In mid-January, we flew to Bolivia together with confidence, faith in God, and a chess set, which we set up exactly 100 times in the coming weeks in preparation for the thirty-plus mentally draining talks that we anticipated.

While my heart beat for Peru, Markus was inclined towards Bolivia and was hoping we would find a suitable location in the Bolivian Andes. For ten days we negotiated with government representatives and church leaders in La Paz, Cochabamba, Sucre, and Potosi. Wherever we presented our plans for a mission hospital, there was great enthusiasm. We left Bolivia in a somewhat confused state of mind and continued our journey to Peru.

On January 23, we were welcomed to Abancay by Dr. Allen George and his wife, Amy. This American missionary doctor had read the English version of our project proposal and was willing to help advise us in the search for a suitable location. He had been carrying out medical operations in the mountain villages for several years, and knew the people and the country well.

That evening, we put ourselves up at a cheap hotel. I was tossing and turning, unable to sleep. Our trip was almost over and the location question was still unresolved. I was afraid of making the wrong decision, and equally afraid of returning to Ecuador without having made a decision at all. How earnestly I desired a clear sign from on high. Markus and I prayed frequently before our meetings and also analyzed each one after its conclusion. We realized that a decision needed to be made – and soon.

After breakfast, Allen picked us up in his 4x4. Our first stop was the Quechua settlement at San Luis, a dismal place 10,000 feet above sea level. The village chief had called several hundred residents to gather on a field. The men stood in a large group on one side, while the women in their colorful costumes had settled themselves comfortably on the grass. I explained our vision in Spanish, and a pastor translated into Quechua. Despite the Indios' eager anticipation, I was skeptical. An icy wind blew incessantly, and the high altitude would not be conducive to our patients' convalescence. After sharing a meal of guinea pig, we excused ourselves politely and drove down into the valley to Curahuasi.

This small town was embedded in a high valley. White anise fields stretched over idyllic mountain slopes. The mild climate was similar to that of a European spring day. On the way to Abancay, I had noticed a sign with a red cross by the road. I had thought it must mean that there was already a hospital nearby, and therefore no need for the mission hospital we planned to build. The existing "hospital" turned out to be a crumbling medical station, providing only the most basic care. As Allen, Markus, and I stepped into the station, I was overcome with absolute certainty that this – Curahuasi – was the place where we were to build. On this beautiful patch of land not far from the Apurímac River, we had finally found what we had been looking for for so long.

The first thing we needed to do was inform the mayor of our plans. We quickly found the town hall near the central square, and introduced ourselves to the newly elected Julio Cesar Luna. He was in his thirties and bubbling with energy. I placed a fifteen-page manuscript (in Spanish) on his desk and briefly explained why we had interrupted his afternoon schedule.

As he grasped the full extent of our plans, he beamed at us in pure joy. What he had just heard must have seemed like a gift from God Himself. He promised us whatever assistance we might need, then hurried back into a meeting.

Unable to contain his excitement, he surprised the waiting dignitaries with the incredible news that some Germans were going to build a modern hospital right in their backyard. They stared at him wide-eyed, probably doubting their new mayor's sanity.

On January 29 we met the president, the director, and the treasurer of the Evangelical Church Council of Peru in Lima. This was followed by talks on February 3 with the Peruvian Minister of Health, Dr. Carpone Campoverde. In both meetings, we presented Curahuasi as the official site for our mission hospital – an idea which met with universally rich approval. We returned with a confidence that far exceeded the timidity with which we had departed Shell in mid-January. We had succeeded in our quest and settled some major questions, but there was one element of sadness clouding our journey: one of our chess pieces had got lost.

15

Worthy of
The Guinness Book of Records

Anybody familiar with South America knows that you can never get anything done in just a week. As soon as official contracts are involved, it can be months before they are finalized. But a week was all that Olaf Böttger and I had to get not one, but *four*, documents prepared and authorized. We met at the airport in Lima on April 7, 2003. I had flown in from Ecuador and Olaf from Germany, carrying $25,000 from various benefactors for the purpose of purchasing a plot of land for the hospital. We flew on to Cusco, then took a cab to the state of Apurímac. The settings for all our activities would be Abancay, the capital, and Curahuasi.

The town officials had selected eight lots for our consideration. Together with John Walter of Constructec, we painstakingly inspected each one. Some were too small, others too difficult to access, and most of them too expensive anyway. To cut a long story short, we were down to a choice between the only two with any degree of feasibility. The owner of one of them was asking an exorbitant price, so the decision was essentially made for us. The chosen plot of land belonged to the Catholic Church, and consisted of six anise fields arranged in a triangle. This had been the option we were hoping for all

I HAVE SEEN GOD

along, as the breathtaking view of the snow-capped mountains from the site was absolutely priceless.

We immediately contacted Padre Tomás, who had responsibility for the bishop's legal matters.

As time hurried by, we tried to work on several fronts at once. On April 8, we completed the paperwork required by the State Health Department in order to give some legal status to the hospital.

On April 10, we had assistance from attorney Efraín Caviedes on the next document. As he busily crafted the statutes of our Peru-based support organization, Olaf crashed out in the hotel room with jet lag. Several times each hour, Efraín would explain something to me, or ask a question regarding the details and purpose of our work. On critical points, I would wake Olaf to ensure we had consensus. It is said that one should sleep on important decisions – apparently Olaf was taking that advice to heart! By 2 a.m. we had worked through twelve pages of jumbled legal jargon. Just a few hours later in Abancay, we solemnly signed the articles of incorporation that would elevate Diospi Suyana to the legal status of a statutory institution.

On April 12, we signed a $60,000 development contract with Constructec. We knew that we would be spending all of the existing Diospi Suyana money on the plot of land, but we had time to raise additional funds before the contract start date of January 2004.

We held several rounds of negotiation with the Catholic Church regarding the purchase price of the selected lot. No one in the capital seemed really to believe that the hospital would be built. But the prospect of receiving $25,000 in cash from a German investor as well as the risk of missing out on a rare opportunity, should the hospital succeed, left the Church with little wiggle room. On April 15, we reached an agreement with Padre Tomás, who had received approval from the bishop to proceed with the transaction. Together with Allen George, we counted out $25,000 in bills onto the cashier's desk at the Banco de Crédito. For the first time in its short incorporated history, Diospi Suyana became the owner of real estate in southern Peru.

Even though the time pressure had meant we couldn't always be as thorough as we would have liked, the four documents were complete and binding. When Padre Tomás heard of our great success, he said it was worthy of inclusion in *The Guinness Book of World Records*.

Olaf and I were both glad and grateful for what had been achieved. We had been juggling far too many balls in the air, and yet managed not to drop a single one. Trusting in God, we were committing ourselves to a course that, from a human standpoint, was absolutely impossible. But, praise God, the word "impossible" is just not in His vocabulary.

During this short but jam-packed trip, we made another decision. Our official logo was adopted, and remains the image of Diospi Suyana today. Three professional designers had drawn up thirty possible drafts, which we deliberated on for hours at organizational meetings. In the end, ten were shortlisted. Olaf and I carried out surveys among numerous Peruvians, from simple farmers to the mayor of Curahuasi himself, showing them the prototypes and tallying their responses to each. In the course of this informal selection process, one motif emerged as a clear favorite: a yellow sun with a red cross superimposed on the lower right side. We were extremely satisfied with this result. The yellow sun represented the culture of the indigenous Andean people, and an expression of our appreciation of the Quechuas in

89

particular. The cross of Christ symbolized God's love to all people. Soon our new logo decorated a thousand flyers and appeared in the newspapers. There was a universal sense that the design was exactly as it should be.

16

Indoor Camping

As we said our goodbyes to our colleagues in Shell, Dr. Roger Smalligan found words of encouragement to share with the hospital staff: "The Johns are planning to build a new hospital in Peru," he said. "With God's help, all things are possible!"

But the look on his face belied the confidence of his words. As the medical director of a mission hospital, he could appreciate perhaps better than anyone the magnitude of the project. He could not say where the millions of dollars and necessary volunteers would come from. To be honest, neither could Tina or I.

With over fifty boxes and suitcases, we moved 1,500 miles south from Ecuador to our new home in Peru. The drive from Lima to Curahuasi was especially memorable. All of us were packed like sardines into the cab of a truck, enjoying the incredible mountain landscape, the shaggy llamas in the pastures, and the one-legged flamingos by the lakes. Despite the splendid scenery, the twenty-two hour journey was admittedly difficult, particularly for the children.

We arrived in Curahuasi at about one in the morning. During a previous visit, Tina and I had purchased on old adobe house in the center of town for about $11,500. Exhausted, we dragged our belongings into the house, and then made our

91

way to the Hotel Santa Catalina. The view from the window the next morning revealed yet another picture of the abject poverty of the mountain farmers in their unplastered mud houses. Tina in particular was deeply moved by the wretched living conditions displayed before her.

We moved into our own home later that week, laying three mattresses on the floor of our future living room to have enough space for all of our sleeping bags. As previously arranged, a construction team from Abancay arrived to renovate the whole house in time for Christmas.

As we were hitting our heads on the ceiling of the top floor, the whole roof had to be raised by about six feet. New doors, windows, and wooden flooring were also part of the plan. We were hoping that the dark, filthy hole under the stairs could be transformed into an attractive, clean shower. The foreman could see no problem with completing the renovation as scheduled, if not ahead of schedule. In fact, he expected the team to have enough time to complete the original contract *and* take on the additional tasks of razing the mud ruins behind the house and erecting a secondary two-story cement or adobe structure.

Their optimism was contagious. With the prospect of having our own cozy home so quickly and so affordably, we were willing to put up with temporary inconvenience.

The construction team arrived on a Monday morning. Within half an hour, our home had been turned into a shambles. While ten men worked from sunrise to sundown, producing unimaginable quantities of dirt and debris, we retreated to the confines of a single room and waited for the dust to settle – literally as well as figuratively.

For furniture, we used the boxes that Tina had stacked up against one wall. Our sleeping area looked like an indoor campsite. The worst thing, however, were the bugs, which plagued us with numerous bites. We all subsequently developed infections that by November required antibiotics to control them.

In the third week of November, Mayor Julio Luna informed us of an imminent visit by the Peruvian Minister of Health, Dr. Alvaro Vidal Rivadeneyra. He was coming on November 20 to see our hospital project for himself. The time of his arrival was not specified.

Early in the morning of that fated day, a representative of the municipal government pounded impatiently on our door. "The Health Minister is coming!"

The news sent us into a frenzy. All decked out in our best, we stood with the mayor and his advisors by the side of the road, waiting to give this prominent dignitary a worthy welcome. But contrary to our expectations, the convoy raced through Curahuasi without stopping, and carried on to Abancay. Disappointed, we changed back into our regular clothes. But not for long. At 10 a.m., we heard that the Minister would be arriving around noon. We again donned our "finery" and stood peering expectantly towards the Pan-American Highway. By 2 p.m., we realized it had only been a rumor. This time, we hung our Sunday clothes back in the closet, almost as a matter of routine. In the course of the evening, the police caught the message via radio that, on his return journey to Cusco, the Minister would indeed be making a stop in the anise capital of the world. We all stood together on the road for the third time that day, determined to stop the motorcade in front of the restaurant at the entrance to town, whatever the cost.

Lo and behold, around 8 p.m., the crowd began to stir. The Minister had finally arrived. He entered the restaurant and

I HAVE SEEN GOD

was shown to the table specially prepared for him. I was given the floor and explained our plans for the mission hospital, using a laptop presentation. Had we been able to show the Minister the actual site during the day, he would have seen only bushes and cacti. But through computer simulation we could give him a much clearer picture of how we envisioned our dream structure.

As one might expect from a politician, he delivered a short impromptu speech of thanks and wished us well with our project, handing Tina and me temporary work permits valid for six months. This was a kind gesture, even if it was purely symbolic since the hospital did not yet exist. Overjoyed, Tina and I thanked God for the positive note on which the day had ended.

In South America, there is often a significant discrepancy between promising and doing, planning and implementing. The construction work on our home had been under way for a month now. As November came to an end, we saw that our Peruvian crew had seriously underestimated the time needed for the contracted renovations. They would not even manage half of what they had promised.

Shortly before Christmas 2003, we left Curahuasi, leaving behind the mess of unfinished construction we called home. The work would need to be resumed as soon as we returned from Germany. When would that be? We had no idea. Tina and I were set to begin a lecture tour throughout Germany, sharing our life vision and attempting to raise support. No one could predict when or how the finances, staff, and equipment would be found to build a new hospital.

One morning before our departure, I was reading Psalm 40. Verse 3 says: "He put a new song in my mouth, a hymn of praise to our God. Many will see and fear and put their trust in the Lord."

As I placed a bookmark in the page, I started thinking. Would our story be so exciting that one day many would want to hear it? Could the tale of Diospi Suyana possibly become the chronicle of a modern-day experience with God? So far, we didn't have much to show except a very bold plan. But deep within me, I sensed that these promises from God's Word would be fulfilled in our lives – in a way that would take our breath away.

17

A Marathon Through Germany

Back in Wiesbaden, we returned to the same tiny loft apartment that Tina and I had shared sixteen years earlier as newly-weds. Since then we had blossomed into a family of five, as Florian Tim had been born in Shell in 2000. So we now had a total of three children, each born on a different continent. Natalie could claim to be African, Dominik European, and Florian a genuine South American.

As soon as the Christmas festivities were over, I sat down at my desk to prepare a PowerPoint presentation. For two whole weeks I compiled and arranged photos to compose the story and vision of Diospi Suyana. I prayed for God's inspiration each step of the way. The presentation needed to provide the facts, but more than anything, it had to reach the hearts of the audience.

Olaf Böttger and I discussed our plan of attack. We needed a brochure that would convey a serious and credible image. We had already had boxes of flyers printed, ready for distribution. We wanted to establish our own foundation. And of course, we hoped for favorable press coverage. On December 30, our local Wiesbaden newspaper published a long article on page three, with the headline: "Task of a lifetime: Wiesbaden doctors to build mission hospital in southern Peru, seeking support."

My parents, Rudolf and Wanda John, and their four children in 1963: Gerlinde is standing in the middle at the back, with me in front of her, and our brother Hartmut on the left and our sister Helga on the right.

Above left: Even as a child I dreamed of a life as a doctor overseas.

Above right: Martina and I at the age of eighteen. From the start we had one goal: "We are going to study medicine and then work as doctors in the Third World!"

Bottom right: Martina, seen here at the age of twenty-five: I was determined to marry her.

April 1987: I completed my studies at Harvard University. I am third from the left.

Our wedding on August 1, 1987 in Wiesbaden.

In spring 1991 we traveled together throughout South America for three months, spending most of our time in Peru.

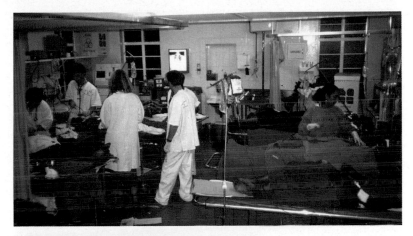

Top: The emergency room at Baragwanath Hospital, at the gates of Soweto.

Left: My patient (third from right) survived a deep stab wound to the neck.

Bottom: From 1998–2003 we worked at the Vozandes del Oriente Hospital in Ecuador.

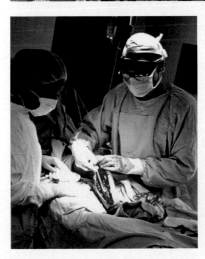

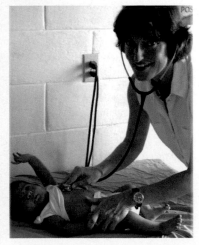

Top: Founding members of Diospi Suyana on August 18, 2002.

Above: Martina John at the kitchen table late at night. We sent out 540 newsletters to friends all over the world with the news: We have taken the big step.

Right: Our move to Peru in October 2003 (here at Quito airport). We had sent most of the boxes on ahead.

Top: View of the plot selected for the hospital.

Left: In the fall of 2003 we settled in Curahuasi, Peru, sleeping for months on mattresses on the floor of a mud house – the only Caucasian family among 30,000 Quechuas.

Bottom: Between January 2004 and July 2014 Martina and I gave 1,880 presentations in nineteen countries.

Top: Presentation in a church in Berlin Schönefeld. The presentations became the basis of our public relations work.

Middle: On May 23, 2005 we raised the heavy construction sign in the middle of nowhere.

Bottom: The German Ambassador, Dr. Roland Kliesow, performed the ground-breaking ceremony. Dr. Victor Arroyo, Director of the National Evangelical Council of Churches, is on the right. I am next to him, applauding.

Left: 3,000 Curahuasinos, including many school students, celebrated the ground breaking.

Middle left: In November 2005 thirty pastors gathered to help build the amphitheater.

Bottom: The hospital construction site, managed by Udo Klemenz.

Udo Klemenz and his wife, Barbara, lived in Curahuasi for thirty months to supervise the construction of the hospital.

Lyndal Maxwell and my wife started the first Kids' Club in Curahuasi in November 2005.

Right: Mine owner Guido del Castillo read a report about us and became a faithful supporter of the mission hospital. He donated the cement and then the roof for the hospital, and even paid for the first well in Abancay Province.

On the threshold of 2004, we looked towards the future admittedly with some anxiety. Germany was in the midst of an economic crisis. Unemployment was up around 10 per cent, and polls showed that every fourth German citizen was afraid of losing his or her job within the next six months. In short, conditions were not ideal for fund-raising! From a human perspective, we were doomed to failure. But perhaps these adverse conditions would serve as a backdrop against which God would show His very real presence.

On January 16, Tina and I gave our first presentation at a high school in Frankfurt. The pile of notes we held betrayed the fact we were not yet fluent with our material. Taking turns, we commented on each of the pictures that were displayed on the screen. Over fifty students paid rapt attention, and our dream of building a hospital for the descendants of the Incas became theirs for an hour. Much encouraged, we packed up the projector and screen. If our story was enough to captivate teenagers spoiled by TV, it must have a fascination all its own.

Ten days later, I addressed five people in the living room of a private home in Siegen. Twenty-four hours after this, I spoke to an audience of nine in Handewitt Ellund, near the Danish border. We were always on the road, sometimes even with the children. By the end of June we had done eighty talks in twelve different German states. Whenever I gave the presentation on my own, I would drive home the same night no matter how far it was. The next morning, I would be back at my desk, calling churches and clubs to arrange more appointments to share the presentation. Some days, I managed as many as seventy long-distance calls. At the same time I was tracking donations, which unfortunately were only trickling in. In the first six months, we received just 251 gifts.

Tina was working just as hard. If she was not with me on tour, she was taking care of the children, who were all attending German school for the first time. She ran the home by day, and wrote to friends and supporters by night. By the end of the year she had written over a thousand thank-you notes. We were both getting very little sleep. If the dream of Diospi Suyana were to fail, it would not be down to laziness on our part.

The more we could share our vision via print media, interviews, and presentations, the more we were committing ourselves to its success – putting all our eggs in one basket, as it were. There were always ups and downs along the way, but this initial six months of striving with all we had in us, and seeing so little in return, was truly a journey through the valley of tears. By June 2004 the sheer magnitude of the project was reducing us to feelings of hopelessness and failure, and the weight of this burden was almost unbearable. We might almost have given up at that point, but we hung on, hoping for a miracle – the big breakthrough…

18

The Big Breakthrough

In the first week of February, fifteen of us from the Diospi Suyana organization met at a retreat center in Thuringia. We knew where we wanted to go, just not how to get there. In a short talk, I reminded everyone of the legacy of Eric Liddell. "The Flying Scotsman" was a runner who, in the 1924 Olympics, made his infamous decision to not participate in the 100-meter dash – which he was favorite to win – because it was being held on a Sunday. He wanted to honor the Lord's Day, and not even the British royal family could convince him otherwise. Liddell did have the opportunity to participate in the 400-meter race a few days later. In the few remaining seconds before the starting shot, someone handed him a note which read: "He who honors me, him will I honor," referencing a verse from the Old Testament of the Bible. Just under a minute later, Eric Liddell amazed the world, passing the US favorite and taking the gold medal for Great Britain.

Referring to this historical event, I encouraged my friends at Diospi Suyana, "If we openly confess our God in our public relations work, even if it causes resistance, He will honor us and the hospital will be built."

I am not the sentimental type, but at that moment, tears welled in my eyes.

On April 15, Tina and I found ourselves in an attractive house in Kleinmachow, in the southern suburbs of Berlin. Gathered in the living room were the senior manager of the Berlin Chamber of Commerce, a TV producer, the wife of a senior consultant physician, and a number of others associated with the upper echelons of society.

Our presentation to them earned exuberant praise: "A fascinating project!" "Fantastic!" "Congratulations on such a good idea – but why do you keep mentioning your faith in God?"

Our distinguished audience was of the opinion that we could believe whatever we liked – as long as we kept it to ourselves.

"You are in Germany to raise funds. You will complicate things for yourselves if you keep bringing 'God' into everything!"

This unleashed a fascinating debate that continued late into the night. "If you carry on like this," these elites warned, "you'll never be able to present your project on network TV!"

Less than twenty-four hours later, Tina and I were on stage before a full house at the Orangerie in Brandenburg. Our presentation was recorded by a network TV team and broadcast throughout the week as part of the daily newsreel report.

There was no doubt: Tina and I gave it everything we had. But it was others working quietly in the wings who were pivotal to our success. In October 2003, we had sent out letters to friends all over the world, telling them of our upcoming fund-raising campaign in Germany. Our plea for help reached a former student, Dr. Gabi Risse. She responded, "I am setting up an opportunity for you to share your presentation in my town of Traben-Traben, on the banks of the Mosel."

And she followed through, hanging the posters herself, notifying the press, and inviting her patients and colleagues to the event, which was to be held in the local Protestant church. She caused such a stir that Diospi Suyana became a frequent topic of conversation in many homes. Dr. Barbara Meinhardt from a nearby Catholic parish also heard about the mission hospital, and without ever having met us, she wrote to the editor of *Family* magazine, Martin Gundlach.

At her suggestion, he invited us to Witten for an interview. He intended to allocate half a page of the August edition to our story. Accompanied by our children, we spent two hours in his office. When he saw our laptop presentation, he was stunned. He too had caught the "Diospi Suyana Fever."

Family magazine is published quarterly and reaches a readership of 150,000 in Germany. What had started as a sidebar article had now morphed into the focal theme of the next edition. Martin dedicated six full pages, complete with photos, to the story "Doctors' Family Drawn to the Indios." He placed another photo on the cover of the magazine, and, in his editorial, encouraged readers to support Diospi Suyana.

In order to make the most of the opportunity, we recruited twenty friends in Wiesbaden to help place money transfer orders in 50,000 flyers that would be inserted into the copies of *Family*. Both Tina and I were beside ourselves with nervous anticipation. Was the big breakthrough just around the corner?

The day the magazine came out at the end of August, we sat at home on tenterhooks. What happened next exceeded all our expectations. Overnight we were catapulted to new heights.

Thousands of readers throughout Germany saw photos of our family in the ruins of a mud house in an Indio village. The pictures and report had an electrifying effect, and the echo of response was overwhelming. Over $75,000 in gifts poured in, and many people committed to regular financial support of Diospi Suyana. We had requests for presentations from just about everywhere, and our calendar filled up in no time. The article in *Family* was followed by others. *The Daily Post*, the only Catholic newspaper in Germany, ran an excellent article entitled "Good Samaritans in the Andes."

Although our story was initially carried primarily by Christian media such as Bible-TV and the *ideaSpektrum* magazine, that all changed in the second half of 2004. In addition to many local newspapers, the national women's paper, *Bild der Frau*, and even the esoteric magazine *Body and Mind* picked up our story. In October, the major European TV network, Sat.1, broadcast a six-minute report, which included a live interview.

In comparison with the first half of the year, financial gifts were up 500 per cent. This encouraged Tina and me not to relax, but to step up our efforts even more. Not one stone had yet been moved in the construction of the hospital, and yet already hundreds of thousands of people were now aware of it. As TV presenter Andreas Malessa laughed, "There was never so much cackling before an egg was laid!"

19

That's Who You Need to Talk to

There are three things you need if you want to build a hospital: money, staff, and equipment. In our search for suitable medical instruments, a company in the former East Germany made us a surprising offer in April 2004: they would completely equip our hospital with used equipment at a cost of $2 million.

I was skeptical. First of all, we didn't have 2 million dollars to spend at this time. And second, I had the absurd idea that one day German companies would supply our hospital with brand-new equipment – at no charge.

We experienced one such thrill in March 2004, when Dr. Kursatz, an anesthesiologist at the Horst Schmidt Clinic in Wiesbaden, called me to say, "Dr. John, we are taking some of our anesthetic equipment out of service. If you want, you can have four sets!"

And oh, did I! Detlev Hofmann, of the medical supply company Stoss Medica, came by with a company truck and helped load up the equipment. When I asked Ms. Teichmann from hospital administration what the value of the equipment was, she replied, "Only about $1.50 – we wrote it off a long time ago."

When Detlev Hofmann aided us, his boss, Axel Lantsch, gave him his complete support. He was a former Boy Scout, and opportunities for helping others seemed to always be on his radar. Just a few weeks before, in the Evangelical Free Church in Wiesbaden, we had shared our presentation with an audience of around 160. In the front row of seats, four people seemed to be paying particular attention: Axel Lantsch, his wife, and their two children. At the door, he shook my hand. "Dr. John, I will help you find the equipment you need. Come by my office and we'll talk about it."

In the German states of Hesse and Rheinland-Pfalz, Stoss Medica is a major supplier of medical equipment to hospitals and doctors' offices. Determined to open doors for Diospi Suyana in the industry, Axel sent out an informative letter to all the medical technology corporations in the country. His message was essentially this: "I am sponsoring the construction of a hospital in Peru – and so should you!"

This opened the door for me to share my presentation with several of these companies.

Mr. Schmitz, of Schmitz and Sons, and his business manager, Mr. Ingermann, were my only audience members when I arrived at the office in Wickede. When I posed the question of whether he could give us four new operating tables, Mr. Schmitz responded enthusiastically, "Yes, Dr. John, you can have them!"

The package that the company ultimately put together for us was worth over $200,000 and consisted of operating tables, patient transporters, stretchers, and furniture.

In the summer of 2004, my mother saw a report on TV about Ludwig Georg Braun, head of the German Chamber of Trade and Commerce. "My boy, *that's* who you need to talk to!"

Since even one's own mother can make good suggestions, we tried various means of requesting an audience with Mr.

Braun. No luck. In the end, Axel Lantsch got involved. Using his business contacts with Aesculap Inc. in Tuttlingen, which belonged to the Braun-Melsungen Group, we finally met with success. On October 27, Germany's top industrialist received our small delegation, consisting of Axel Lantsch, my wife, and me, for a ninety-minute appointment.

The meeting had been prepared with military precision and took place in a friendly atmosphere. Yet, as Mr. Braun made no concrete promises at that time, we drove back to Wiesbaden somewhat disappointed.

We could not have predicted the magnitude of the eventual results of our short visit that day. In the spring of 2005, Ludwig Georg Braun authorized the donation of hundreds of thousands of dollars' worth of surgical instruments through Aesculap. He further arranged for the provision of a two-year supply of vaccines and medication through the Braun satellite in Peru.

In the fall of 2005, Axel Lantsch and his family emigrated to Australia, and he became an inactive stakeholder in Stoss Medica. For eighteen months of our journey, he had been indispensable to Diospi Suyana. As he packed his bags, I was full of concern. He had done so much – how would anyone ever fill his shoes? I need not have worried. Other companies were stepping forward, and we were slowly but surely acquiring all the equipment we needed.

I HAVE SEEN GOD

20

The Kaltenbach Story

Shortly after the report in *Family*, Pastor Günter Born of Lörrach called us. We knew him from the old days and were glad to hear from him. "I'm afraid we can't commit to supporting you financially on a regular basis," he said sheepishly, "but we are going to be advertising your work downtown!"

At the end of the week-long advertising campaign, I was to go and personally share the presentation at their church. Whether or not the campaign had been a success, I was in no position to judge. On the evening of September 28, about forty people gathered in Pastor Born's church to hear more about Diospi Suyana. They gave a good offering and promised to send more. I drove back to Wiesbaden and fell into bed exhausted at 2 a.m.

As I was tracking the list of financial gifts on the internet the next morning, I noticed a surprisingly large amount from a name I did not recognize, so I called the bank and asked what city the gift had come from. A friendly lady told me that the gift's origin was the town of Lörrach, and she wished me luck with my search. Now that I knew the name of the donor and their city of residence, I was able to look up the phone number I needed.

When I called, a woman's voice answered: "Kaltenbach

residence."

"My name is Klaus John. My wife and I are the originators of Diospi Suyana. We just received a rather astonishing monetary gift. Is it perhaps from you?"

"Yes, it is." Mrs. Kaltenbach did not expound further.

"Were you at my presentation in Lörrach last night?" I really wanted to get to the bottom of the matter.

"No. What presentation was that?"

This genteel benefactor in Lörrach was a puzzle to me. "So why did you send Diospi Suyana such a large gift?"

"I recently read an article about you in a family magazine. And there has been talk of nothing but Diospi Suyana all over Lörrach this entire week!"

I finally had my answer, and thanked her sincerely for her incredible generosity. A brief internet search revealed that the Kaltenbach family owned a large company that exported metal saws worldwide.

In the second week of October, I was scheduled to talk about Diospi Suyana to a missionary organization in Switzerland. My destination was Zurich, which meant I would be driving right past Lörrach on the way. On the spur of the moment, I called Mrs. Kaltenbach and offered to share the presentation with her and her family in the privacy of their living room that Saturday morning. At first she was hesitant, but she eventually accepted.

Holding a large bouquet of flowers, I rang the doorbell at 10 a.m. The Kaltenbachs and their four children welcomed me so warmly and the atmosphere was so friendly that I ended up staying for over three hours.

"So," Mr. Kaltenbach said when I had finished my slides, "you should actually come and share this again at my Rotary Club."

That was music to my ears!

Then Mrs. Kaltenbach joined in the brainstorming. "At Christmas, we usually organize a fund-raising concert in the evangelical church. Diospi Suyana would be a great cause!"

They sent me on my way with their best wishes and a sack of walnuts. That informal meeting in the Kaltenbach living room bore much fruit. At the Christmas concert, Tina and I gave the presentation to a packed church and were presented with an offering of $3,000. The Rotary Club sent us over $7,000. The Kaltenbach–Diospi Suyana axis became stronger and stronger. On one of my many return visits to Lörrach, Mr. Kaltenbach shared another idea he had had: "With our company network, we could provide the equipment for the hospital repair shop!"

The brilliance of that suggestion was immediately obvious.

"I know the chief editors of the leading regional newspapers," he continued. "We'll run a series in the press!"

As always, Mr. Kaltenbach kept his word. Two of his employees were freed up to take care of acquiring and reconditioning the equipment we would need. The daily press in southern Baden regularly published detailed reports on the "repair-shop project," which soon had an estimated value of almost $80,000.

After an information meeting at Christ Church, which turned out to be more like a press conference, Mr. Kaltenbach and I stood in the foyer chatting. "Dr. John, I recently went skiing with the head of the Sandoz Group. You two really should talk!"

My thoughts entirely, but the portfolio I had sent to Sandoz the year before had undoubtedly ended up in the trash unopened. However, with Mr. Kaltenbach's support, my chances were much better this time round. Exactly ten days later, I was received by Andreas Rummelt, head of the Sandoz Group, and Anne Schardey, who ran the Public Relations Department. They absorbed my introduction to Diospi Suyana in this meeting that my comrade Kaltenbach had so remarkably made happen.

"Dr. John, you communicate a great deal of enthusiasm for this work. What is it we can do for you? Do you need money? Medication?"

Of course, I had anticipated Mr. Rummelt's question.

"Would you consider sponsoring the construction of our intensive care unit?" I asked timidly.

"How much would that cost?"

Mr. Rummelt's kind face gave me the encouragement I needed. I drew a deep breath and replied, "$80,000."

"You'll be hearing from us."

Sandoz transferred this exact amount to the account of Diospi Suyana. Following my presentation to 150 Sandoz employees in the canteen, members of the PR department gave another $8,000. The Sandoz Group sent an additional $15,000 in January 2009, as well as nearly $30,000 worth of medicine and a commitment to continue supporting Diospi Suyana in the future.

What was it Pastor Born had said? "I'm afraid we can't commit to supporting you financially on a regular basis, but we are going to be advertising your work downtown!"

The end result of this "small project" was now close to $280,000. Tens of thousands of people had taken part in various fund-raising events benefitting the mission hospital in Peru because of the advertising Pastor Born had provided. What a mysterious chain of events – the "new normal" at Diospi Suyana. How can one explain such things? Even the most die hard agnostics struggle to find a logical rationale, but eventually they have no alternative but to consider the metaphysical. For Christians, it is so much easier. They say, "God has provided..." and fold their hands in thanks.

21

At the European Parliament

We were slowly beginning to think about our return to Peru. But who would look after our financial supporters? Who would be the point of contact in a future Diospi Suyana office? Several people had applied for the position, but Olaf, Tina, and I could not come to a consensus. In the summer of 2004, we discovered Anette Bauscher from Solms, who had ten years' experience in the public relations office of a Christian media company. As cordial as our talks were, they ended in a stalemate, as Ms. Bauscher was not interested in moving as we requested to the Rhein-Main or Darmstadt area, where the support organization was registered.

On September 1, we traveled to Brussels to present our project to Hartmut Nassauer, leader of the Christian Democrats in the European Parliament. The meeting was a disaster. We were told point-blank not to apply for any funds whatsoever from the European Union. "There is way too much red tape – do not waste your time. Petitions of this kind drag on for years and have a highly uncertain outcome!"

During our six-hour drive back, the three of us had plenty of time to talk. By the time we climbed out of the car at home that evening, we had reached a decision that had nothing to do with the European Union in Brussels. We had decided to offer Anette Bauscher the job whether she was willing to move or not.

My phone call to her at 9 p.m. was not at all expected, but the way had been paved. Earlier that same day, Ms. Bauscher had asked God for a new job. And now, just hours later, one was being offered to her.

Since January 1, 2005, Anette Bauscher has been an invaluable addition to Diospi Suyana. For the most part, our trip to Brussels did not go at all as we had hoped, but she is the reason we can look back on the venture fondly. At the end of 2012 she oversaw a perfect handover of the work to Erika Alex. In retrospect, Anette Bauscher contributed immensely to the success of our ministry.

22

Cogs in a Large Wheel

As February 18, 2005, approached, I anxiously anticipated the arrival of the two executives from Constructec who would be coming to Germany from Ecuador to negotiate the details of a construction contract with Diospi Suyana. I felt that I must have my head in the clouds. In the first year of our concentrated fund-raising effort, Tina and I had received $500,000 in gifts – not a bad start, but only a drop in the bucket of what would be needed. The contract stated that the building costs of the hospital would be well over $3 million. That was just for the building itself and did not include anything inside: equipment, furniture, etc.

I estimated the value of the requisite equipment to be about $2 million. But it was not only money we were lacking. Something else was becoming an even bigger headache.

For months I had been looking for an engineer to oversee the construction work in Peru – a man with international experience, who was healthy and strong, and willing to move to Peru for two years. We were also hoping to find someone who would do all this for nothing. Maybe there was no such person. If there was, we definitely hadn't discovered him yet.

Two days before the meeting was scheduled to take place, I was sitting in our tiny loft apartment. Next to me at the table, attorney Klaus Schultze-Rhonhof was attempting to explain the fifty pages of "legalese." The initial draft of the contract contained many terms that were totally incomprehensible to me as a doctor. Mr. Schultze-Rhonhof had offered to assist me with the negotiations with Constructec. All my hope rested on him, for, as "luck" would have it, Olaf Böttger fell ill that week and was unable to participate in the talks with Constructec.

"I too belong to a charitable organization," the attorney said, pushing his notes to the side a bit. "There are about twenty of us, and we raise funds for the children of prostitutes in São Paulo, Brazil."

Klaus Schultze-Rhonhof and I were on the same wavelength; I could feel it. His humanitarian efforts piqued my interest. Then he continued, "One of our group used to be an engineer for Philip Holzman."

I remembered that Philip Holzman had been one of Germany's leading construction companies before it went bankrupt. The man he was talking about must have a working knowledge of the construction business!

"May I ask his name?"

"Of course. His name is Udo Klemenz. He lives in Solms, near Wetzlar."

"You wouldn't happen to have his phone number, would you?"

My voice conveyed a sense of urgency. The attorney bent down and rummaged in his briefcase under the table. A few minutes passed, and it looked as if he would come up with nothing.

"Here it is!" he cried with satisfaction, and passed me a small scrap of paper.

"Would you mind if I gave Mr. Klemenz a quick call?"

"Not at all," the attorney replied, shaking his head. "Maybe you'll be in luck and he'll be home."

A deep voice answered the phone.

"Mr. Klemenz?" I asked, trying to sound friendly.

"Yes, how can I help you?"

"We are a small group of doctors and nurses who want to build a mission hospital in Peru. We are looking for a civil engineer who could supervise the work." I knew there was no point beating around the bush so I took a deep breath and asked the boldest of questions: "Can you imagine doing the job – for nothing?"

I held my breath, waiting for his response. Truly, my request was nothing short of laughable. My words must have sounded both naïve and presumptuous.

"Yes, I could imagine doing the job," he said. "It would be best if you could come by and discuss the matter with my wife and me in person. How about this evening?"

"That works for me!" I almost shouted, flabbergasted. I remembered my manners, thanked him politely, and promised to be in Solms at 7 p.m. on the dot.

As I hung up, the attorney commented dryly, "Dr. John, you are just the man for this!"

After this affirmation, we turned our attention back to the draft contract.

With a press of a button, I turned off my GPS. So this house on the hill was where the family lived. During the one-hour drive from Wiesbaden, I had tried to imagine what our meeting might be like. Would they be at all interested in our hospital in Peru? Full of hope, I rang the doorbell.

Udo and Barbara Klemenz were of course expecting me. They ushered me into their living room and helped me set up the projector and laptop. My Diospi Suyana presentation lasted about an hour. Word for word, I repeated for the 250th time Tina's and my life story, which flowed, as always, into the evolution of our daring dream, the dream of building a modern mission hospital in the Andes. The Klemenzes followed along in silence.

Surprisingly, it was Barbara Klemenz who spoke first. Her few sentences left me speechless. "My husband and I are committed Christians here in our local Lutheran church. For the past three days, we have been wondering whether God might have a special task for us to do."

A shiver ran down my spine, and I tried to contain my excitement.

"We have prayed many times for God's guidance," Barbara Klemenz continued. "When you called this morning, my husband and I were sitting in the kitchen, thinking about the direction of our lives. Your call was like divine guidance!"

Then it was her husband's turn. "I worked for Philip Holzmann for thirty-five years, thirteen of which were in developing countries." He cleared his throat. "I have the experience you are looking for. The timing of your call this morning seems to indicate that God wants us to go to Peru!"

The drive back to Wiesbaden took far too long. I couldn't wait to tell Tina what had just transpired. It was obvious that God had acted in an incredible way. When Tina heard, she was so moved she could not speak. Then she said, "We are all cogs in God's big wheel!"

Negotiations with Constructec began as planned on February 18, and lasted four full days. Joining us at the table was Udo, who had become a cornerstone of Diospi Suyana overnight.

23

Seeing It Through

A few weeks later, Udo and I flew to Peru together. It was my tenth flight to Lima. I hadn't slept a wink the night before; instead, I was firing off a barrage of emails to South America so that the coming days would be as productive as possible.

The outcome was indeed spectacular. Between April 7 and 15, the two of us gave the hospital presentation thirteen times, during which we made the acquaintance of the following dignitaries: Dr. Roland Kliesow, the German Ambassador to Peru; Dr. Pilar Mazzetti, the new Minister of Health; Ms. Suarez Aliaga, the President of the Federal State of Apurímac; and Dr. Victor Arroyo, the Director of the National Council of Evangelical Churches.

On April 15, I gave the presentation three times to the leading Peruvian newspapers. *El Comercio*, *La Republica*, and *Perú. 21* each published detailed reports and made Diospi Suyana known to a very wide audience throughout the country. While I was giving my speech, Udo was busy taking pictures with his digital camera. Although he did not yet speak Spanish, he soon proved his exceptional intelligence as he pieced together odd words, snatches of conversation, gestures, and body language to decipher the outcome of our meetings. He was usually right on target.

In addition to all the presentations, we of course made time to visit the future construction site at Curahuasi. But first, we made a stop at the town hall to see Mayor Julio Cesar Luna. He gave us a most cordial welcome and spontaneously called a meeting in his office. His advisors, together with some women and children, squeezed up on the hastily arranged chairs in order to catch a glimpse of the developments displayed on the laptop screen. This presentation was for the very people who would one day benefit from the hospital. The pictures conjured up a prospect that seemed too good to be true.

"Dear Curahuasinos!" I said in conclusion, looking around the room at the twenty or so people gathered there. "It is time. In May, we begin."

In the eyes of my audience, I read a mixture of amazement and doubt. No one said anything as they waited for their mayor to take the floor. According to the dictates of protocol, he would now respond in long, flowery sentences. Mayor Luna stood up and took a deep breath, but he was unable to speak a single word. He tried again, but his voice broke. Someone passed him a tissue so that he could wipe the tears from his face. He finally regained sufficient composure to be able to make a suitable remark. But in actuality, his tears said far more about what our hospital would mean for the people of Curahuasi than any speech could ever have done.

The next day, John Walter of Constructec flew in from Quito to plan the next steps with us. We all holed up in the Hotel Catalina. After years of planning and hypothesizing, we had now reached the time for action. We sat in my room and talked deep into the night about the initial construction work that would follow the ground-breaking ceremony.

Mr. Walter, a US citizen, had spent ten years in Ecuador and had largely assimilated into the Latino culture, adopting the typical mindset. No matter what potential difficulty we brought up, he dismissed it as no problem. Everything could be worked out. Starting from scratch, he conjured up an impressive plan of action that Udo Klemenz did not take entirely seriously. We were both concerned about whether or not we should be trusting someone like John Walter with the construction. But Constructec had done the planning and we knew no other construction company in the area, so, by all indications, we really had no choice.

During the night before we left, we three had an unusual "bonding experience." The water supply in Curahuasi had been cut off, and unbeknown to him at the time, Udo had not turned the faucet off all the way. Just before midnight, water flooded through the pipes once more. It was not long before the sink was overflowing. Udo was sleeping soundly and did not notice that the water level in his room was creeping up inches by the hour. Half asleep, John and I could hear the sound of water splashing, but we thought it was the rain outside. By the time John banged on my door, the water was already flowing across the hotel corridor. We would have to act fast to avoid severe damage to the hotel. Our shouts woke Udo, who jumped out of bed only to find himself ankle-deep in cold water. We eventually got the embarrassing situation under control with pails, scrubbing brushes, and rags – John and I in fits of laughter at Udo's expense. Fortunately, he didn't hold this against us.

In mid-April, we returned to Germany. The orientation trip had been a final rehearsal before the ground-breaking ceremony took place on May 24. Immense logistical challenges lay ahead, and our finances were very tight. After months of fund-raising and numerous presentations, Tina and I had raised $600,000. As we were working without the financial backing of the German government (or Bill Gates), and without any kind of loan, we were well aware that each new day could be the project's last. Nevertheless, we were anxious to see the bulldozers roll in – and we kept up hope that in some miraculous way, financial giving would keep pace with our expenses. From a human standpoint, our plan was totally crazy. Without God, it was simply impossible.

24

WANTED: Warehouse

U p to this point, we had been storing the equipment donated to the hospital for no charge in a small warehouse owned by Stoss Medica. "Just for a while," as I kept saying. I did not want to abuse Mr. Lantzsch's generosity. Besides, we were soon going to need a much bigger warehouse to store the remainder of the equipment until it could be packed for shipment to Peru. I estimated we would need about a 3,000-square feet space, but there was no way we could afford the $3,000 per month for rent. With building due to commence, we needed every cent we had.

I inquired at various freight companies. None of them seemed to have any available space. But that was no surprise, as we wanted it rent-free. Understandably, they were not lining up to miss out on $36,000 of annual rental income! Our appeals via our website and newsletter yielded no response. Perhaps there was space out there somewhere, but no one let us know.

As long as friendly hands were willing to squeeze our boxes into the shrinking space at Stoss Medica, I didn't lose too much sleep over our storage conundrum. However, the grace period ended suddenly in mid-May, when I received a call from Mr. Hoffman. "Dr. John, you really must move your items immediately. Our warehouse is bursting at the seams!"

"Yes, we are looking for an alternative." My answer was truthful, but unfortunately there was no alternative in sight.

I discussed my predicament with Helmut Steitz. We had worked together with the church youth back in the 1970s and 80s. As an employee of the State Ministry of the Environment and Conservation, he had some interesting contacts. I was soon granted an appointment with the head of the state government's real estate department.

The bureaucrats were surprisingly "unbureaucratic" and offered me the vacant Land Registry Office in Dieburg, south of Darmstadt. We really had no time to lose, so Axel Lantzsch, Olaf Böttger and I met a few days later to check out the property. A friendly government employee was there to meet us. Unfortunately, the space was completely unsuitable for our needs. The narrow rooms did not offer any storage space for bulky medical equipment. There was no ramp to get into the building. The upper floor was accessible by stairs only. How could we maneuver our heavy items, some weighing more than a ton, up and down? In addition, the building was not secure. Although we certainly appreciated the generous offer, our faces fell in disappointment as we walked through the rooms. This would not be the workable alternative we sought.

"Why don't you ask at the Schenck Industrial Park in Darmstadt? They have large warehouses!" The government employee meant well, but the lead was less than promising. I had already asked so many companies, and had been universally turned down. With our obvious options still exhausted, we said our goodbyes and drove home.

Still, our days at Stoss Medica were numbered. We had to investigate every potential solution, so I went ahead and called Schenck. The phone was answered by someone who gave me an address to which I could submit my request in writing. I sent a letter as directed, and followed up a week later by phone. To my surprise, I was put through to the Head of Administration, a Mr. Pfuhl.

"Dr. John, I have read through your petition. I can see how passionate you are about your hospital project," he said, and then paused slightly.

I was bursting with impatience.

"But I am afraid I cannot offer you anything at all," he continued. "All our warehouses are full."

My shoulders sagged in disappointment. Yet there was something in his voice that gave me hope.

"Mr. Pfuhl, you just have to help me. I have been trying to find storage for months. I don't know what else to do!" My voice was a clear distress call.

"I'd like to help you, but I can't."

Mr. Pfuhl was no doubt sympathetic to our cause. He did not speak as though he were trying to brush me off. So I did not let go.

"Mr. Pfuhl, please don't leave me hanging. We are really in a mess!"

"I might have a basement of 900 square feet, but that would be too small for you anyway."

I pricked up my ears. Was this a straw to grab onto?

"Fantastic! We would be grateful for anything you could give us!"

Perhaps I was a bit too euphoric, as Mr. Pfuhl tried to get my feet back on the ground.

"You fly to Peru first for the ground-breaking. Then we can talk again the first week of June."

25

Joyous Celebration

I arrived in Curahuasi the day before the ground-breaking. I was not alone. Jörg Bardy and his wife, Birgit, from Lüdenscheid had also booked tickets to Peru to see for themselves what was unfolding there. They were considering coming long-term to serve as physical therapist and general practitioner respectively. When they heard this historical ceremony was to take place while they were in the country, they caught a connecting flight from Lima so they could participate. Gynecologist Dr. Jens Hassfeld and his wife, Damaris, left their three children behind in Germany while they came to take a closer look at their future workplace. It was a kind of "second honeymoon" for them, and I joked with them about having nothing but romance on their minds. The Australian radiologist Lyndal Maxwell joined us, traveling down from Ecuador. With US doctor Allen George, his wife, Amy, and the social worker, Hannelore Zimmerman, we made a total of nine – the inaugural cadre of Diospi Suyana.

The dry season had begun, and the snow-capped mountains rose majestically into a radiant blue sky. But I was tense. On the construction site, there were only bushes and undergrowth – nothing that would suggest that a major proceeding would be taking place there in less than twenty-four hours. We were expecting at least 3,000 people, including the German Ambassador and the Director of the National Council of Evangelical Churches, who were traveling all the way from Lima.

Around noon, we erected a large sign displaying the mission statement of Diospi Suyana in bold, black letters: "With this hospital, we want to honor God and serve His people in Peru." We noted the end of April 2007 as the projected date of dedication.

After lunch, John Walter climbed into a Caterpillar and appeared to have a blast flattening an area for the big event. There was no sign anywhere of a stage, but the town council workers had unloaded trunks and boards, presumably with that end in mind.

"Everything will be ready for tomorrow!" they promised, and leisurely began work on assembling the scaffolding that would serve as a platform.

Tuesday morning began with singing, for the German participants. We practiced the German national anthem, just in case, and then made our way to the site where amazing things had happened overnight. A 60-foot-wide stage stood in the right place, and it was decorated with hundreds of balloons in the national colors of both Germany and Peru. Canopies on either side would provide protection from the glaring sun for Curahuasi's distinguished visitors.

A weight was lifted from my shoulders as I saw that the German Ambassador and the Director of the Council of Churches had arrived on time from Lima. Long processions of Curahuasino pilgrims made their way towards the town. Several school classes marched to the site, bands playing alongside. Their colorful uniforms added to the dignity of the setting. In the meantime, a spokesperson from the town administration was busy warming up the crowd. He fired off witticisms into the microphone: "This hospital in the anise capital of the world will be the best, the most beautiful, the biggest in Peru!" He seemed to have an endless supply of superlatives. The churches in the area had made giant posters displaying their response to the hospital project. One such banner conveyed a particularly poignant view: "The Diospi Suyana Hospital is God's gift to Curahuasi!"

The dignitaries, including a beauty queen from Cusco, were called up to the stage individually, amid great applause. Soon, the representatives of the church and the regional and municipal governments were all seated beside the missionaries, one in purpose. To me, it was absolutely incredible. Three years ago, Tina and I had sat at a desk in Ecuador writing a proposal for the building of a mission hospital, and now here we were, crowded together with thousands of people who evidently believed in our vision. They belted out the Peruvian national anthem as their flag was hoisted high, and rejoiced as the German Ambassador joined us in singing the German national anthem as well.

In my speech, I quoted a few verses from the Gospel of Luke. Jesus had begun his public ministry with an announcement of His purpose: "The Spirit of the Lord is upon me, because He has anointed me to preach good news to the poor. He has sent me to proclaim freedom for the prisoners and recovery of sight for the blind, and release for the oppressed."

The German Ambassador stressed the point in his address that the German staff would be working side by side with the Curahuasinos in the future, a statement which resulted in thunderous applause.

It was probably the few words shared by Dr. Allen George that touched the most hearts. He told of his wife Amy's brain tumor, her two operations, and the uncertain outcome of the disease.

"I have learned," he said into the microphone, "that the only things in my life that are of lasting value are the things I have done for God!"

Two folk-dancing troupes brought the old Inca culture back to life, reminding us of the origin of the people we would serve.

The highlight of the ceremony was of course the groundbreaking itself. We had intentionally included the Catholic Church and the regional authorities. There must have been doubts whether this colorful media event would ever be followed by the actual construction of a hospital. The flamboyant rhetoric of Peruvian politicians often rang hollow: much was promised but little was ever delivered.

But we were Germans, and it seemed the "Alemanes," as we were called, could be trusted to do just about anything.

26

Arrow Prayers on the Highway

No sooner had I unpacked in Wiesbaden than I had a call from Mr. Hofmann.

"Dr. John, you need to have your belongings out of our warehouse by Thursday. Is that clear?" he asserted, straightforward and uncompromising as usual.

I was not slow to understand. His message was received loud and clear! I still had forty-eight hours until his deadline, and planned to visit Mr. Pfuhl in Darmstadt the next day.

On Wednesday, my GPS took me unerringly to Darmstadt, and to the gates of the Schenck property. I had used the journey down for several quick, in-the-moment "arrow prayers." At the gate, I was given a visitor's pass and was escorted to Mr. Pfuhl's office.

"How nice to see you!" Mr. Pfuhl was ready to go. "I'll just call Mr. Weg, our custodian, and then we'll take a look at our options."

Mr. Weg's easy-going, personable manner impressed me right away. The three of us set out to take a look at the warehouse, taking the elevator down to the basement from one of the back buildings.

"Here we are!"

Mr. Weg unlocked three rooms. I could see they were all clean, dry, and secure. Mr. Pfuhl had indicated on the phone that all three were available for a certain period of time at no charge. A huge weight had just been lifted. After being turned away so many times in the last few months, I had at last found what I needed here at Schenck.

"Mr. Weg, what else do we have to offer Dr. John?"

Mr. Pfuhl's question was completely unexpected. I tuned in a little more carefully, and did my best to appear agreeable and innocent. It seemed our walk through the complex had only just begun. We crossed several halls and finally came to a halt in front of two large rooms, each about 1,700 square feet.

"He could have these two rooms as well," Mr. Weg proffered, a suggestion which met with his supervisor's full approval.

"That is over 3,000 square feet all together!" I exclaimed in incredulous gratitude.

"Could well be," murmured Mr. Pfuhl, who was visibly pleased by this positive outcome. "So, the storage space is yours for a year!" he said, patting me on the back. His eyes sparkled with the mischievous satisfaction of a Boy Scout who has just done his good deed for the day.

I could have shouted for joy all the way home. There was now nothing to stand in the way of an immediate transfer of the donated equipment from the Stoss Medica warehouse to the Schenck property. For two whole years, as many as ten container loads were stored simultaneously at the Darmstadt facility. The rental costs waived can only be estimated – somewhere between $80,000 and $150,000.

"Going the extra mile" is a saying that was to be proved most profoundly between Mr. Pfuhl of the Schenck Company and Diospi Suyana. What had started out as an offer of 900 square feet expanded exponentially to 12,000 square feet in just a matter of months.

27

Emigrating to Peru

Four weeks after the official ground-breaking ceremony, construction work commenced under the supervision of John Walter. Of course, it was a massive undertaking for him to launch a project of this magnitude up in the Andes, so far from Lima. His first step was to walk the streets of Abancay, inspecting local construction companies. Abancay is almost fifty miles from Curahuasi, across a mountain pass at 12,000 feet. The round trip takes about three hours. The photos that John had emailed while we were in Germany showed endless lines of men on our site, looking for work. But no real progress seemed to be being made. It was time for Udo and me to get involved.

On August 3, 2005, a small crowd gathered in the departures area at Frankfurt Airport. Five members of the John family and two Klemenzes were being seen off by family and neighbors. There was an undercurrent of excitement, such as one might experience before heading off on expedition. We were not leaving for a beach vacation on the Adriatic, but were about to become real-life pioneers in the Andes. The historic group photo shows thirty expectant faces. One enthusiastic young lady is holding up a wooden sign with a yellow sun and a red cross: the Diospi Suyana logo.

The flight to Peru via Atlanta was uneventful, and as soon as we arrived in Lima, we settled into a guest house run by a Swiss missionary society. We were not putting down roots there, just staying long enough to take care of our visas, get our Peruvian drivers' licenses, and prepare for the remainder of the journey to Curahuasi. One such related task was to purchase a Hyundai 4x4. I went with Udo in search of a roof rack a couple of days later. We understood that a part of the city called Victoria was the best place to find auto accessories of all kinds.

We were just driving along the broad avenida when an agitated middle-aged woman flagged us down. About 100 yards further along, a man standing on the left side of the road looked at our car and shook his head, an expression of pity on his face. Had something come loose on our Hyundai? We stopped to check it out.

Right then an auto mechanic, who must have been covertly waiting nearby, crawled under our vehicle and reappeared with hands covered in oil. From his torrent of words, we grasped that he was telling us there was something seriously wrong with the car, but we were at a loss as to what it might be.

"I know a good repair shop nearby. I'll take you there!"

Our "guardian angel" climbed in and directed us around several corners. "Here we are!"

We knew right then that we had been had. We were in a rundown area of Victoria, surrounded by a bunch of people who were all yelling at us, gesticulating wildly. It seemed that the 4x4 was completely shot, but each of them somehow had just the part to fix it.

Udo and I realized we had run into a trap set by a car gang. I was suddenly filled with a sense of alarm. To make matters worse, the car would no longer start. Had these con artists messed with the engine and made it unfit to drive?

While Udo stuck close to the vehicle, I ran onto the street and yelled for the police. A patrol car arrived within a few minutes and two officers with rather bored expressions on their faces climbed out.

"Calm down!" one of the officers said. "They only want to steal your car."

His words did little to allay our concern.

"Please get us away from here!" we urged them.

"Be glad to!"

One of the uniformed officers got in the back of our car and instructed us to follow his colleague's vehicle. Miraculously, the engine started this time, and we got away from that dangerous area as quickly as possible. In no time, we reached the *Comisaria*, the local police station.

"We got you out of that pit back there, and now we expect a little thanks!"

We were taken aback by the policeman's brazen presumption. As if to clarify what they wanted, the officers held out their hands. I placed a ten *soles* bill in each of their outstretched palms and muttered "Thank you" in Spanish. But the two sergeants shook their heads vehemently. "That is not enough!"

That's when I lost it. Angrily, I pulled a newspaper article about Diospi Suyana out of my pocket and explained to them through gritted teeth that we were building a hospital for the poor in Peru and did not deserve to be exploited by highway robbers or corrupt policemen. The police did not attempt to counter my outrage, and we left without further incident.

28

In the Mire of Corruption

U do Klemenz looked out at the flattened building site, his feelings of discontent plainly visible on his face. There was a conspicuous lack of steel, cement, and other tangible elements of progress here. It was almost December 2005, and our supporters in Europe were hoping to *see* some of the effects of their contributions: foundations, walls, and such. But what did we have to show? Holes. Nothing but holes.

Three months had gone by since our return to Peru. Udo Klemenz was still waiting for the construction plans from Constructec.

"John, how am I supposed to do my consulting work if I have no plans?"

Udo's frustration with the lack of necessary documents did not seem to bother John Walter in the least. He usually responded casually, "Next Tuesday. Or in another week!"

His commitment to any kind of planning was extremely tenuous, a good intention at best. Unfortunately, he had turned out to be a fountain of empty promises. The organization of this project was slipping through his fingers.

Several of the local pastors asked to speak to me. They brought a series of accusations against John that sounded so outrageous that I had difficulty taking a single one of them seriously. But if there was even a shred of truth in any of these charges, not only was the reputation of Diospi Suyana at stake, but we might eventually find ourselves in court because of some of Constructec's dealings. We were all very concerned.

Tina and Barbara Klemenz met regularly for prayer. For this particular situation, Barbara began to pray: "Lord, let everything that is hidden be brought to light!"

She had prayed this ten times at the most when things started to change.

It was Saturday. Pay day. Around noon, I drove to the construction site.

"Have you got your full pay?" I asked some of the workers who were just leaving.

They shook their heads angrily. "No, Constructec always pays late!"

There was a gnawing feeling of suspicion in my gut. Were the pastors' terrible allegations going to turn out to be true? I had to take action, and fast. John Walter was in Quito that week, so I could not confront him immediately. But maybe his absence was a good opportunity to investigate the complaints against him.

I summoned the senior engineer from Constructec and the payroll administrators to meet at my house at 2 p.m. Andres Murillo, John Walter's right-hand man, was also in attendance. We sat around the kitchen table, tension etched onto everyone's face. As if it were an interrogation, I questioned everyone. It was not long before Murillo and his people had become so entangled in their conflicting stories that a whole mess of financial infractions were brought to light.

Later that afternoon, Udo Klemenz, two pastor friends, and I discussed the best plan of action. We now had every reason to fear that more of the accusations against John Walter and Constructec might be true.

In the evening, we drove up over the pass to Abancay for the purpose of conducting our own investigation. For days, we questioned witnesses and compared all statements until, finally, pieces of the puzzle began to come together to form an extremely disturbing picture.

John had kept company with some pretty shady characters, and repeatedly behaved in a manner contrary to good morals and ethics. His escapades in the red-light district and his drinking bouts in public came as quite a shock to us. In addition, he had not complied with the legal requirements for hiring workers. Andres Murillo turned out to be a real crook as well, and it was relatively easy to see this with the facts we had. Although diesel was available much more cheaply at the gas station near the building site, he had been transporting fuel all the way from Abancay, purchased from a merchant who overcharged, and then provided him with a "kickback" under the table. We estimated he had pocketed close to $5,000 as a result of corrupt practices such as this. We very quickly learned how the South American "good ole boys" functioned. Andres Murillo was a legend in the "network," as illustrated by the impressive police record we had been anonymously given.

We attempted to summon John Walter from Ecuador first by email, then by phone. We considered how best to proceed. Should we seek to have him arrested as soon as he set foot in Apurímac?

Finally, John replied that he was on his way, presumably to expose all rumors as slander. The night before he was to arrive, I sat at my desk until dawn, compiling a summary of all the evidence we had gathered to date. With our closest friends, we prayed constantly that God would resolve the whole predicament and keep Diospi Suyana from any further harm.

John Walter was accompanied by an attorney from Lima. We were joined by our attorney, Efrain Caviedes, from Cusco. The situation was grave. Depending on the outcome, this crisis could mean the end of Diospi Suyana.

As John Walter looked on defiantly, it was agreed that I should begin the meeting by reading my list of grievances. Item by item, I presented the details of our concerns, corroborated by the results of our investigation. In the face of such evidence, there was little argument to be made. As I finished speaking, John broke down and made a full confession.

Several days later, we received forty invoices on which John had very obviously forged the figures. As a result, he was banned from the work site. His business partner, Carlos Pullas, was designated to pick up the remainder of the project in his stead. All dealings with Andres Murillo were terminated immediately. The Peruvian workers were then employed legally and paid on time from that day forward. Just as Barbara had prayed, everything came to light.

Constructec was held liable for all financial damage sustained. Not one cent of the generous gifts given to Diospi Suyana was squandered. In fact, none of our supporters even knew how close to destruction our dream of a modern hospital for the Quechuas had actually come.

29

Hurdles and Dead Ends

Despite our chronic lack of funds, the walls of the hospital slowly began to rise. The more comprehensive the work became, the more complicated the logistics. What we really needed was an efficient computer hook-up. Our mayor, Julio Cesar Luna, did in fact have an internet connection at the town hall, but data transmission was so slow that one could almost starve to death waiting for information to come through. The town's telephone network consisted of nine coin-operated phones. Anyone needing to make a call had to wait in a long queue. Once on the line, the sound transmission delay and the constant static made it very difficult to understand the person on the other end. Coordinating work between the construction office in Curahuasi and the suppliers in Lima was a nightmare. Contact between Peru and the Diospi Suyana office in Germany was even more so. The area did not have any cell-phone towers so there was absolutely no mobile service on the 300,000-square feet construction site. Each element of communication inefficiency was inconvenient and frustrating on its own; put together, they created a maddening quandary that needed a solution quickly.

Perhaps Telefonica could assist. This telecommunications giant from Spain enjoyed quite a monopoly in Peru at the end of 2005. I made several attempts to set up an appointment with the directors in Lima. I was hoping they could run a phone line right onto the hospital site and set up an internet satellite dish.

Thanks to Dr. Roland Kliesow, the German Ambassador, I was finally able to talk with Telefonica. Since his participation in the ground-breaking ceremony, the Ambassador had shown himself to be a true friend to Diospi Suyana. Whenever possible, he used his considerable influence to open doors for us. On November 17, 2005, he personally accompanied me to the headquarters of Telefonica, where he had arranged for us to meet three company directors.

My distinguished audience was polite, though somewhat distant, as they followed my presentation about Diospi Suyana. When I asked them to support our project with a satellite dish, they asked for a map of Peru. They had never heard of Curahuasi, and it was suddenly clear to them why.

"Curahuasi is miles away in the mountains," they grumbled. "That must be over 600 miles from Lima."

Their interest in helping us, if it had been there at all, vanished in that second. The Andes have been a forgotten region for centuries, and still are. Many Peruvians demonstrate more concern over the welfare of their pets than over the Quechua people.

"We will see what we can do for you."

South Americans do not like to say no. They prefer to put things off until they are forgotten. As the Ambassador and I took our leave, I seriously doubted we would get much help, but I refused to give up hope completely.

A few days later, I boarded a plane once again. I was heading back to Germany to continue sharing the vision of Diospi Suyana across the country. These trips were turning into strenuous tours, with me cramming up to fifty presentations into a three- or four-week period, and driving anywhere between 6,000 and 10,000 miles. My chronic fatigue made the night-time journeys particularly dangerous, and I often wondered how I had stayed free of accidents and illness during this time. It can only have been the prayers of many, many people.

On December 19, 2005, I arrived back in Peru at midnight. Exhausted from the flight and the marathon tour, I wanted nothing more than to go home to my wife and children, and prepare for Christmas. I cleared Immigration and headed to Customs, where I handed in my form, on which I had checked "Nothing to Declare," and pushed the button. Anyone who has traveled to Peru will be familiar with this drill. Once the button is pressed, either the green or the red light comes on. If it is red, all bags and suitcases are opened and carefully inspected.

"No big deal," I thought to myself as the red light blinked on. "My bags are easily opened and closed."

"What have we here?" a rather grumpy Customs officer asked, pulling my digital projector out of the bag.

"I use the projector during the presentations I do to raise money for humanitarian aid. We are building a hospital for the Quechua Indios."

The woman did not buy my explanation at all, and was determined that she had caught a smuggler trying to sneak an electronic device into the country that night. When I finally made it out of Customs, it was 2 a.m. and I no longer had a projector. I was eventually told that I had failed to check the required box on the Customs forms. I was extremely annoyed. I had heard lots of horror stories about Lima Customs Control, but had hoped to avoid ever becoming entrapped myself.

After Christmas, I began in earnest to try to get my confiscated projector back. Several officials from the Ministry of Health intervened. The Director of the Council of Evangelical Churches and finally even Dr. Kliesow, the German Ambassador, advocated strongly on my behalf. As a result of their efforts, I was invited to a meeting with the Directors of Customs for Airfreight in their offices on February 1, 2006. I finally had an opportunity to demonstrate the truth I had been stating all along. Of course, I also shared the Diospi Suyana presentation. What more convincing way was there of showing that my projector had served only a noble purpose in the last two years? After all, the hospital would be helping the poorest in Peruvian society.

The next week was etched on my memory as a time of extreme frustration. Customs decided not to return my projector. It had probably long since left the Customs Department anyway, via the back door, and was irretrievable. It is said that troubles never come alone, and true enough, I received more bad news that same week. An officious female voice informed me by phone that the directors of the telephone company had declined to support our work. There would be no satellite dish for Diospi Suyana at this time.

My efforts with Telefonica and then Customs had taken up weeks of my time. I had invested hours in my presentation in Lima, and in letters and phone calls. I had absolutely nothing to show for any of it. As a very goal-oriented person, I found this very difficult to tolerate. I was resigned to my fate, but as a Christian, I also asked God WHY.

I wandered aimlessly through the long streets of Lima. I felt totally empty, disappointed, burned-out. That week, I posted an update on the Diospi Suyana website entitled

"Dead-end Lima." The accompanying photo showed a dark, canyon-like street going nowhere. Actually, it was a view of my heart.

30

An Amazing Turn of Events

I had to get another projector, that much was clear. I already had forty presentations scheduled in Germany for March and April.

"Buy one in Lima," Olaf Böttger recommended, "then you won't have problems with Customs again."

At the Swiss missionary guest house in Lima, I leafed through the Yellow Pages. There were surprisingly few companies in the capital that sold projectors. On February 10 I set out to compare different models and prices. Rush-hour traffic, the famous *hora punta*, was just beginning when a cab dropped me at the address I had selected. I rang the doorbell and took stock of the building. It looked more like a private address than a store.

A young Peruvian opened the door and led me along the hall to a room of considerable size, obviously set up for demonstrations. Several technicians were sitting at a large table, heads bent over various electronic components. A screen hung at one end of the room.

A man in his mid-thirties introduced himself as the owner.

"My name is Passalacqua. How can I help you?"

His encouraging smile and quiet manner filled me with confidence.

"I would like to buy a 2,000 ANSI lumens projector. What do you have to offer?"

The company had a number of different models available. I narrowed the list down to two, and got out my laptop to test both projectors with my presentation. Unlike at some of my more recent showings, everyone here seemed genuinely interested in the story of Diospi Suyana, putting down their work and focussing their complete attention on my slides. One of the last slides showed a photo of me with the German Ambassador during our visit to Telefonica.

"Unfortunately, that visit didn't get us anywhere," I commented dryly and clicked to the next photo.

After my run-through, a man addressed me unexpectedly. He must have been standing in the corner behind me, because, despite his size, I had not noticed him at all.

"Is it true that Telefonica won't help you with such a great project?" he asked, incredulously.

"Yes, unfortunately," I answered. "We just got a firm refusal this week."

"Maybe I can help you. Here is my business card."

To my amazement, he gave me his card with his contact details printed in clear, blue upper-case letters: DANTE PASSALACQUA, PRESIDENT OF IMPSAT. The man in front of me was about forty years old, was a relative of the owner of the company from which we were seeking to purchase the projector, and, it seemed, had just happened to stop by for a visit.

"We sell the same equipment as Telefonica," he said. "And by the way, next time you are in Lima, please come by and share your presentation with my board of directors!"

Three weeks later, I took a cab to the office on Avenida Olguin. Huge antennae on the roof of the building and a large sign with "IMPSAT" printed in large letters let me know I was at the right place. It was located in the southern part of Lima, near the "Jockey Plaza." At the adjacent racetrack after which this sprawling shopping mall was named, noble steeds belonging to the few rich people in this city of 8 million would race against each other. The audience in the stands would place bets on the horses, assuming they had any money left after they had paid the entrance fee. It was widely known that the Peruvian soccer star, Claudio Pizarro, kept his horses at stables here. But that was not what was on my mind as I approached the large complex of buildings on my right.

An elevator took me to the fourth floor, where Mr. Passalacqua and two of his managers were already waiting for me. It just took a few seconds to hook my laptop up to the projector on the table. The gentlemen gestured for me to begin. If there is such a thing as a wave of compassion, one could feel it as I shared the Diospi Suyana story yet again.

No sooner was I finished than Mr. Passalacqua turned to his colleagues, speaking slowly as he struggled to maintain control: "I told you the pictures would get to you."

Then he turned to me and presented me with a prepared document already bearing his signature. As my eyes skimmed over the text, he summarized the contents.

"We will donate a satellite dish to Diospi Suyana and install it free of charge on the construction site. The equipment supports international telephone calls and efficient internet connectivity."

Passalacqua was obviously pleased to be the bearer of such good news.

"Our gift," he continued slowly, "is worth $25,000 per year and is not time-limited. As long as IMPSAT is operating in Peru, our promise will remain."

Then it was my turn to struggle for words. The whole scenario was like a fairy tale. I had lost my projector at Customs. That had been irritating, BUT, as a result, I now had a new satellite dish for the hospital – a resource that would ultimately save us hundreds of thousands of dollars.

The laws of probability could not account for this miracle. Nothing could, but the hand of God. My joy knew no bounds.

Nobody had any way of knowing that this mysterious tale had by no means come to its conclusion. In fact, it was just getting started.

31

The Amphitheater

No one remembers just whose idea it was, but in retrospect the suggestion to build an amphitheater was a stroke of genius. In an area where there was neither movie theater nor concert hall, such a structure would offer interesting possibilities for all kinds of events.

As part of the construction plans for the hospital, Constructec had penciled in a semi-circular area that the ancient Greeks in Athens or Sparta would have been proud of. The sloping ground of the site was perfect for such an arena.

We were hoping to complete this part of the project with volunteer labor, in an effort to keep costs down. Anyone who might have happened upon our site on November 11 would most likely have rubbed his eyes in disbelief – thirty pastors from local churches showed up to haul away rocks. They had hoped to set an example for their church members to follow, and, over the course of the next four months, over 750 of them did.

Usually about twenty men and women would appear at the site on any given morning. They would wash boulders of all sizes, haul in and mix sacks of cement, then put the stones together like a puzzle to form beautiful walls. In a matter of weeks, eighteen rows, one above another, grew up the hillside.

The reward for this back-breaking labor was a glass of the mango juice that Tina was producing by the bucketful.

The open-air theater became an example of good cooperation in every respect. Catholics and Protestants toiled together in the heat of the sun and under the weight of the heavy stones. It also took on an international dimension. The website www.Jesus.de picked up our project and offered to solicit donations online for a full year, bringing in $15,000 in gifts.

"On Saturday, April 23, we need to dedicate the amphitheater," I told the Diospi Suyana team. "I need good photos for my US tour the following week."

My logic did not seem to impress anyone. Maybe the workers thought it was a late April Fool's Day joke. Either way, no one was in agreement with my ambitious proposition.

"Impossible!" said Udo Klemenz. "The stage isn't finished, there are no handrails, the restrooms still aren't functional... and we currently have no money to cover major expenses!"

"Where there's a will, there's a way!" I retorted. "Udo, you will manage it somehow!"

My confidence in Udo Klemenz and the construction crew was well founded, and they did not disappoint me. They built, painted, and sweated deep into the night for an entire week. As the construction team worked around the clock, we gained the attention of local TV and radio stations. Banners were hung over the streets, announcing the event. Invitations went out to VIPs in the state of Apurímac as well as to all the churches in the region.

We hurriedly put together a program that contained a balance of music, speeches, and presentations. In order to ensure that our guests did not go hungry, we calculated that we would need about 500 pounds of chicken, 3,000 sandwiches, and the same number of bottles of cola. But just how many people would, in fact, show up that night, we could only guess. Estimates ranged from 2,000 to 4,000 attendees.

The day before the event, there was frenzied activity. The baker's bread production was delayed by several hours. In the afternoon, when our order had finally arrived, Tina gave the order to start cutting open the rolls – and the whole team pulled out their knives and got to work. In another part of Curahuasi, twenty Indio women were busy stripping the 500 pounds of chicken. As darkness fell, we were still waiting for the truck with the drinks we had ordered. It eventually showed up around 10 p.m.

The great day had arrived! As the first rays of the sun became visible in the sky, the decorating team set to work on the amphitheater itself. Gerhard and Heike Wieland, Tina, our children, and the Klemenzes all passed the lung-function test as they blew up 300 balloons.

The program was scheduled to begin at 1.45. There were only 500 visitors in the amphitheater at this point, but we felt obliged to be punctual. Ready, set, go! In the course of the first hour, the arena began to fill up visibly. By 4 p.m., close to 3,000 visitors were gathered in the giant crescent.

The anthems of Peru and Curahuasi rang out, and soon the celebrations were in full swing. In my address to the crowd, I referred to the amphitheater as an extended hand of friendship. We wanted a message of hope to go out from this place as we trusted in God's presence and love.

The meticulous planning of the program was not at all typical by South American standards, but in some miraculous way we actually stayed on schedule. Three different ensembles provided a beautiful backdrop of music, and encouraged everyone to join in the singing. Then we honored the thirty churches that had sent the 750 volunteers to help build the theater. Each church was presented with a large clock for their building. For twenty minutes, Tina and I shook hands gratefully with the recipients. There was great joy all round.

The mayor of Curahuasi, a representative of the central government, the head of Constructec, and even the Dean of the Association of Lawyers in Cusco were all in attendance, and took the opportunity to say a few words to the assembly.

Following a stirring sermon by a local pastor, a folk-music group began to play, and thirty volunteers fanned out to distribute the food we had prepared. Immediately after eating, about 500 visitors left the amphitheater, leaving no doubt as to why they had come.

At 6 p.m., Tina and I began our presentation of the story of Diospi Suyana. We had given the presentation hundreds of times before, on multiple continents, but this one topped all the rest. Behind us, a 270-square feet screen; above us, the stars; and in front of us, 2,500 enraptured Curahuasinos.

Again and again, we were interrupted by spontaneous applause. As we drew a comparison between Diospi Suyana and Machu Picchu, the audience laughed. But they listened in awe as we shared the miracles God had done in recent months. Nearly 600 people stayed for the movie we showed after the conclusion of the more formal program, but most did have to return to their mountain villages.

At midnight, we dropped into bed exhausted. The next morning, however, we were wide awake as we held that day's edition of *Chaskies*, the biggest newspaper in Apurímac, in our hands. A third of the front page and three more reports on page two saluted the dedication of the Diospi Suyana amphitheater as a major national event.

I HAVE SEEN GOD

32

Twelve States in One Trip

In 2004, Olaf Böttger and I had traveled to the States for a week to found the Diospi Suyana USA non-profit organization in Michigan. Roger Smalligan, our former medical director from Ecuador, had taken on the executive role, and Steve Deters of Jenison had assumed the duties of secretary. On this occasion, we had presented our vision of a hospital for the Indios to the charity committee of Innotec, Inc. Back then, the committee members had nodded graciously, patted me on the back, and then taken their leave of "the crazy dreamer."

Since then, two years had passed. We were now in the beginning of a four-week tour of the US. The first of thirty-five presentations was scheduled to take place on May 1, before the same committee who had rejected our previous appeal for assistance. The evening before, Steve and his wife, Crystal, helped me to polish up my presentation.

"If all goes well," they said, "you'll get $5,000 tomorrow."

Unlike the last visit, it was not computer-animated graphics displayed on the screen, but real pictures of real progress being made on several buildings on site in Peru, and of real equipment being stored in Germany, awaiting transport overseas. The pictures were indisputable evidence that $2 million in monetary and in-kind donations had been contributed to a project they had previously dismissed as unrealistic. Their eyes grew wide and their mouths fell open. Not a single one of them had expected this to happen. In a powerful culmination, I displayed the latest photos of the amphitheater and 3,000 rejoicing Quechuas.

"Dr. John, what you have achieved in Curahuasi is absolutely incredible!" one of the committee members said. "What can we do for you?"

"Well, if you really want to make a contribution," I said deliberately, "you could finance the construction of the hospital chapel."

"How much are we talking about?" came the next question.

"Oh, I think about $100,000 would cover it."

I could not tell you today where I got the courage to ask for such an amount. Innotec had never donated more than $10,000 to a humanitarian project before.

"We will discuss the proposal," was the Americans' friendly reply. They did not seem to have taken offense at my request.

At lunchtime, I was sitting in the company cafeteria, eating with Steve. I could see that he was a bit "unsettled." He obviously had some news that was difficult for him to keep in.

"Klaus, guess what the committee decided!" he finally blurted out.

I could tell from his tone of voice that they had agreed to a gift of considerably more than $5,000.

"I have no idea," I said truthfully.

Steve looked me square in the eye, and slowly enunciated every syllable of an amount that set my heart racing.

"*One hundred thousand dollars.*"

The decision by Innotec had already made my trip to

the US worthwhile before it had really even got going. For the next four weeks, I flew from one state to the next, East Coast to West and back again. I spoke to clubs, churches, and charity organizations, bouncing from airport to car-rental company to hotel. In the remaining thirty-four presentations, an additional $30,000 was donated to Diospi Suyana. I was on the go for a solid month without a break. Of the thirty nights on the road, I got a full night's sleep maybe two or three times.

Arriving home in Curahuasi, I dumped my suitcase and fell into the first chair I found, completely exhausted. I felt like a zombie, wrung out, empty, and so very tired.

33

Red Tape

Once I had got my laptop through the doors and onto a CEO's desk, we could usually count on getting some kind of support from the company, often in the form of discounted prices on needed supplies. After my presentation, thumbs usually went up in approval, and costs went down. I spent a great deal of time on the road, attempting to solicit bargains and to keep the financial obligations of Diospi Suyana as low as possible.

One day in June, Carlos Myasatu, the head of a glass company, allowed himself to be talked into a 40 per cent price reduction on all the window panes for the hospital, cutting his profit by about $20,000, but sharing in a dream that made his heart glad. That same month, a Belgian company, Celima, offered us a 30 per cent discount on its products, saving Diospi Suyana an additional $50,000 on tiles and suspended ceilings.

Dealings with the Peruvian authorities were entirely different, and it seemed that every day brought a new challenge. As a non-profit organization, we were considered exempt from the usual 19 per cent tax, but we were required to pay up front, and then seek reimbursement from the government. The formalities involved in doing this dragged on for six months, a test of patience for us and the other 450 NGOs in the same situation as we all waited for our checks. Our chronic

153

I HAVE SEEN GOD

shortage of funds threatened constantly to bring construction to a standstill, and so I begged the authorities to prioritize our paperwork. With a prayer on my lips, an imploring look on my face, and a natural gift in the art of persuasion, I could often reduce the waiting time by months.

I often had to travel to Abancay for administrative procedures. These so-called *trámites* were a nightmare. No matter how well one might have prepared for an appointment, something would always be missing: maybe an ink stamp, maybe a signature. Always something. In addition, the one person you absolutely had to speak to would somehow never be available: he or she might be traveling, or on vacation, or tending to a relative who had suddenly fallen ill. It was usually best to just marvel at the bureaucratic inefficiency rather than lose control and yell. A fierce look and angry words did not advance your paperwork by a single inch. This was a lesson I had to learn the hard way. However, if you just happened to mention that you had an appointment with the editor-in-chief of a newspaper that evening, everyone instantaneously became much more interested in being helpful...

It is critical to build a positive relationship with "the powers that be." Often a desk photo can be an opportunity: "Is that beauty queen in the picture your daughter? How charming: just like her mother!" You can't go wrong with a remark like that. And if you add that, just last weekend, the Peruvian soccer player Pizarro scored an impressive goal in the German league, a smile of satisfaction will appear on the official's face and your paperwork will smoothly glide from the bottom of the pile to somewhere near the top.

And should your new friend sign off on your paperwork there and then, rather than after a two-week delay, it is absolutely critical to remember to express profuse gratitude, praising the clerk to the skies and shaking his hand with great gusto as an outward display of utmost thanksgiving. Getting annoyed with the "system" does nothing but shorten one's life. Having a good laugh about it all might actually lengthen one's life. But woe to those who get stuck interminably in the tangle of red tape. Nothing can bring down a project faster.

It was already dark by the time I got back from Abancay on the evening of June 22. I knew I would not find anyone still at work on the construction site, but I drove up the rocky approach road anyway, perhaps following an inner leading. Captured in my headlights, I suddenly saw three figures in the entrance area: a man in a floppy hat and two women. Who on earth would be hanging out here so late at night? I rolled down my window and regarded them with suspicion.

"May I help you?"

The man in the hat answered, "We are from the Institute of Culture in Abancay. We have just come to take a look around."

His piercing eyes and tone of voice made me very wary.

"Unfortunately, it seems that Diospi Suyana is not in possession of a license from our Institute," he admonished.

I immediately had a sense of foreboding and unconsciously bit my lip.

"There may be old Incan artifacts buried here. We will be informing you in writing what the fine for digging without proper clearance will be."

And with these unwelcome words, they turned on their heels and were gone.

We had removed almost 3 million cubic feet of earth and had not found even a fragment of a pot. As a result I did not attach any great importance to the matter, and had almost forgotten the incident entirely when an envelope was delivered to our house a few days later. It was from the Institute of

I HAVE SEEN GOD

Culture and looked very official. I opened it and began to read.

I was shocked by the disastrous news contained in the letter. Since Diospi Suyana did not have a license from the Institute to dig, an immediate freeze had been imposed on all construction. A mathematical formula was then used to calculate the amount of the fine imposed for our infraction. I hurried to the site office and showed the letter to one of the Peruvian engineers.

"Robinson, how much do they want from us?" I asked.

Robinson Palacio studied the letter carefully and then answered without any show of emotion, "$700,000."

His response was enough to make my hair stand on end. As foreigners in a strange land, we were about to be run into the ground by ludicrous, impersonal regulations. What did the corrupt officials in Abancay care about the humanitarian aspect of our work? It didn't matter to them that German students and housewives were financing our hospital. All they could see was that there was money to be made from Diospi Suyana.

We had started to build the hospital with complete faith in God. Now people were trying to put an end to our plans. What should we do in this terrible situation? We did the only thing we could: we all prayed. The Bible says that God is only a prayer away from each of us. Sometimes that is never more apparent than when we are facing a crisis.

Three weeks beforehand, on June 4, five Johns, two Klemenzes, and the Wielands had all sat together in front of the TV. At 6 p.m., the newscaster would be announcing the results of the presidential election. Polls had suggested a neck-and-neck finish between Alan García Perez and Ollanta Humala. Humala was running on a nationalistic ticket similar to that of Hugo Chavez in Venezuela.

We were riveted to the screen as the announcement was finally made: "Fifty-five per cent for Alan García Perez!"

The outcome was a relief to us all. After his first unsuccessful period in office in the 1980s, the charismatic leader of the Social Democratic Apra Party had secured a second term. We hoped he would make the most of it.

A few days later, I had the strangest idea. I could not get it out of my head, so I reached for the telephone.

"Ambassador, Sir, could you please help me get an audience with the newly elected President or his wife, please?"

Dr. Kliesow was 650 miles away at his home in Lima and I could only imagine the look on his face as he quickly and emphatically responded.

"Absolutely impossible!" he bellowed into the receiver. "Even I would not be able to get an audience with the Garcías so soon after the election, and I am the Ambassador!"

The brief telephone call to the German Ambassador should have made it abundantly clear to me just how presumptuous I was being. But I couldn't let the idea go, and so that evening, I shot off an email with the same question to Dr. Franzisco Contreras, former President of Ophthalmologists in Peru, whom I had met three years earlier through the Christoffel Mission to the Blind. Dr. Contreras was and still is a gentleman from head to toe, and has the best contacts with the Peruvian upper classes.

I did not have to wait long for his reply.

"Dr. John, I know a lot of people in Peru, but unfortunately Alan García and his wife, Pilar Nores, are not among them."

In the last line of his email, however, Dr. Contreras mentioned a Melitón Arce, who had served as Deputy Minister of Health in García's first administration. He said he would talk to him.

Dr. Contreras evidently kept his word because I soon received an email from Dr. Arce himself. It was only a couple of lines long, and more polite than promising. He did not expect my request to be granted, but he indicated that if I composed a message detailing my petition and rationale, he would forward it to the President himself, whom he had known for thirty years. I thanked him courteously and attached some photos to the message I crafted.

When the phone rang a few days later, it was Dr. Arce's secretary. Her voice sounded most urgent.

"Dr. John, you and your wife have an audience with Pilar Nores de García next Tuesday, July 4. Dr. Arce will also be present!"

I don't play the lottery, but at that moment I felt like someone who had just got all six numbers right. Tina and I did a quick wardrobe check, cleaned our shoes, and booked a flight online from Cusco to Lima for July 3. It seemed that everything in Peru boiled down to politics, and we sincerely hoped that our bold initiative would generate additional support for the Diospi Suyana cause, rather than hinder it further. We left our children in the care of the Klemenzes as we traveled to the capital.

We were pretty nervous as we stepped into the First Lady Elect's office with Dr. Arce. Our presentation would take forty-five minutes, assuming Pilar Nores could allow us that much time. We were optimistic, as we knew she ran a charitable organization called "Sembrando" and was well aware of the problems of social injustice and human need.

As Pilar Nores entered the room, we rose from our seats. The friendly smile on her pretty face immediately put us at ease, dispersing all tension. Following the usual pleasantries,

I HAVE SEEN GOD

we all sat down on the same side of her desk, attention turned to the fifteen-inch computer screen. We were ready to begin.

Tina and I took turns guiding our two spectators through the most important stages of our dream, and showed exactly what had been accomplished at Diospi Suyana in the last four years. Pilar Nores and Melitón Arce appeared to be engrossed in our story, right up to the last presentation slide, which said in large letters: "Would you be willing to become the patron of Diospi Suyana?"

Tina and I breathed a great sigh of relief. We had had the opportunity to say everything we wanted to say. Now the outcome was in God's hands.

The President's wife was visibly moved.

"Yes, I would be glad to be your patron," she said. "And I will help you get the equipment that has been donated through Customs."

The meeting had lasted seventy minutes.

"Actually, it is difficult to account for the fact that we are here together today, so soon after the elections," Pilar Nores said as we prepared to leave. "But my husband asked me to meet you, and it is very rare that my husband asks me to do anything."

As we walked out into the fresh air, appreciating the blue sky that stretched out over the city, Dr. Arce turned to us and affirmed, "Your presentation touched the First Lady's heart."

Tina and I had been eyewitnesses that it had indeed.

The following week, the mayor of Curahuasi and some of his advisors traveled with me to Abancay. We had requested an appointment with the Director of the Institute of Culture. Diospi Suyana had neither complied with the directive to halt construction nor sent any money to the Institute.

As usual, I asked if we could begin the meeting with my presentation. When I had finished, I looked the official right in the eye.

"As you can see, the President's wife is in support of our project and has agreed to be our patron. Do you really want us to stop building?"

"No, no, no, no, no – of course not," the director acquiesced. "Keep going! Your hospital is a fantastic project."

The Institute of Culture had demanded $700,000 from Diospi Suyana. After our meeting with Pilar Nores, the nasty notification of this fine was fit only for the trash can. And that is where it went.

34

The First Container

There had been no lack of warnings. Importing all the equipment that had been donated to Diospi Suyana would be a nightmare, an obstacle course with no guarantee of success. The struggle with officials from Customs for sea and air freight might go on for months or even years.

A Catholic priest once complained to me that he had had to fight for six years to get his church car released from Customs. Horror stories like this were fairly common. And after my own unpleasant experience with Customs inspectors, I could only expect more drama and frustration as we prepared to start moving the equipment over. There were several reasons for this sorry state of affairs, which causes a great deal of damage to Peru itself. The country undoubtedly suffers from bureaucratic overload, and the backlog precludes the timely processing of virtually anything. On top of this, there is near total indifference on the part of many officials in regard to the needs of the people for whom this equipment was being donated. I knew about these hindrances all too well, so I was actively seeking a way to smooth the course for our shipment. The equipment simply had to get to the hospital.

Curahuasi is over 650 miles from Lima. It would cost around $5,000 to transport a freight container from the coast to our hospital in the mountains and back. The thought of using such a large proportion of our financial gifts just to transport goods did not sit well with me at all. In search of a solution, I met with the head of the Lima office of Hapag-Lloyd, an international shipping company, on July 13. Ms. Cateriano, a mature woman of Austrian origin, at first appeared rather aloof. In response to my request to transport and store our goods free, she initially said nothing. Then she referred me to a man whose name was not familiar to me: Carlos Vargas.

Carlos Vargas was the President and CEO of Neptunia, Inc. Its considerable shipping fleet and large warehouses near the port indicate Neptunia's key position in container transport. Ms. Cateriano called Mr. Vargas on the spot and asked him to meet me. She didn't say a word of what it was about.

Carlos Vargas had booked a vacation in the Bahamas for his family. They were scheduled to leave on July 21, but, thankfully, Mr. Vargas found time to see me the day before. As I set up my laptop and projector in the conference room at Neptunia, I was alone, and prayed out loud that God would bless my presentation. A man of about forty years old came in and welcomed me cordially. I once again shared my tried-and-true presentation, and then sat back after the last photo.

"Dr. John, what is it you want from me?" Mr. Vargas asked.

I sensed instinctively that I had been led to the right place.

"Could you store and transport our containers free of charge?"

I always present my requests in a neutral tone, not as a petition, but as an invitation to be part of something great.

"How many containers are we talking about?" Mr. Vargas did not seem opposed to the idea.

"About ten, I should think," I responded and looked at him expectantly.

"Fine, we'll do it. We'd be glad to help you with ten containers."

The Neptunia boss was going out on a limb and verbally committing to a $50,000 gift!

I wished him a pleasant vacation in the Caribbean and was already mentally crafting a headline to announce this fantastic news on our website.

The container with the repair-shop equipment was our "test run," so to speak. Sometime in July 2006, it was due to reach Peru by boat. In the spring, Kaltenbach Co. had arranged for two of their employees to fly out at the end of July and assemble the equipment for us. In all probability, there would be some kind of hassle and delay of the shipment, which would result in the two workers from Lörrach sitting around with nothing to do.

But when we place our trust in God, sometimes things happen in a way that could not have been foreseen. On July 16, we received a letter from the First Lady of Peru, officially confirming her sponsorship of Diospi Suyana. In her letter, Pilar Nores explicitly stated that she would help with Customs matters. Two days later, the ship with our container sailed into the port of Callao.

As usual, almost half a week went by until all the containers had been unloaded and electronically registered on the port's system. Then came the unavoidable "excitement" of the red tape. Roberto, of the Customs agency *Prosoi*, and I attempted to hand in the required paperwork at a counter in the central Customs hall. But the woman at the desk had absolutely no intention of accepting our papers, and told us to come back in the afternoon. More time wasted!

Roberto and I grabbed a phone and placed a call straight to the Customs Directorate.

"We represent the Diospi Suyana Hospital," I told the unsuspecting administrative assistant confidently. "Pilar Nores is our patron, and I would like to request expedited processing of our Customs documents."

I further asked that she be so kind as to call the clerk at the counter and remind her of her responsibilities.

What we had hoped would happen, did. The fact that the President's wife supported us worked wonders all over the place. Within a mere ninety minutes, the first Diospi Suyana container had cleared Customs. (That was certainly an improvement on the six years it had taken the priest's car.) On July 29, a rig belonging to Neptunia drove through the gates of the construction site with the container. The driver had been on the road for twenty hours, transporting our precious cargo up and down the mountains of the Andes. He had set out exactly one week after my meeting with Carlos Vargas.

As I stood ready with a camera and video recorder, a large contingent of volunteers helped to unload the massive machines. A wheel loader belonging to the town administration proved to be immensely useful, and the mayor himself assisted in lowering the heavy components on strong ropes. On Saturday afternoon, I could hardly believe our good fortune. We were ready for the Kaltenbach employees to arrive!

Less than twenty-four hours later, they showed up at the site, dressed casually in T-shirts. They got settled in their hotel and started right on schedule that Monday. This precise timing would probably go unnoticed in Germany, as it is more or less expected. But in South America it is no less than a miracle, and there simply was no human explanation for what had occurred.

35

The Snowball Effect

In the spring of 2006, technicians from IMPSAT had installed the promised satellite dish at the construction site. The hardware, software, labor, and waived connection charges were all a gift of unlimited duration from the company, and worth about $25,000 a year. When the original dish was replaced a few months later with a larger one, the value of the gift essentially doubled.

Such an unusual and prodigious gift deserved some media attention, so IMPSAT notified the press. In June, journalist Doris Bayly from the popular weekly magazine *Somos* traveled to Curahuasi, accompanied by a photographer. IMPSAT had paid for their flights, not entirely for altruistic reasons, since the report would not only cover a German couple's vision, but would also put IMPSAT's gift in the spotlight through both words and photos. Each week, copies of *Somos* change hands many times and are read by over a million people. There was therefore much to be gained from this publicity.

The report, which spanned three full pages, appeared in the September issue with the title: "Angels in the Andes – German Doctors Turn Modern Hospital in Apurímac into Reality." Doris Bayly described in detail what she had witnessed first-hand, and then commented on our project in her unique style, combining humor and sarcasm. One paragraph read, "If the Johns had suddenly decided to travel around the world by scooter, no one would question them. But here they are, step by step, living out their dream of providing long-term help to people in need, when they aren't even related to (Bill) Gates – this makes people think that they are crazy!"

Crazy or not, meeting us apparently touched Doris Bayly's life, and there was no doubt that she was sympathetic to the cause of Diospi Suyana. As she wrote, "It is not every day you hear about a married couple coming to Peru with nothing but their three children and brilliant professional training, and deciding to found a hospital where the poorest of poor can be cared for with dignity and with the help of modern technology." Statements such as these really got to the Peruvians.

Ten days later, a truck with 600 sacks of cement unexpectedly rolled up at the site. Typically, a load like this would cost about $5,000, including transportation. I went up to the driver and inquired about the mystery donor.

"Guido del Castillo sent you the cement," was the brief answer. "He owns a gold mine in the south of the country."

Guido del Castillo, as I soon learned, had read the report in *Somos*. His desire to help us was no momentary whim. A few months earlier, his son had been killed in a parachuting accident. Andres del Castillo's death had opened the eyes of this tycoon to another dimension in which human life and well-being are worth far more than money.

I picked up the phone and thanked him for his generosity. I also offered to give him a private showing of our presentation in Lima. He was very interested, and two weeks later I was striding through the doors of his company, MDH.

Guido del Castillo, his sister, and a handful of other employees welcomed me effusively. Del Castillo was easily over seventy years of age, the lines on his face evidence of a lifetime of adventure. He radiated benevolence and a natural authority.

As I opened my laptop and started my presentation, they all drew in around me, following with rapt attention to see what noble purpose the cement might serve.

"What else do you need?" Guido del Castillo asked as I came to the last slide.

I had been anticipating this question and had an answer prepared.

"Perhaps you might like to supply the steel for the hospital roof. We need fifty-five tons."

The amount I had just mentioned so casually would cost about $70,000 on the Peruvian market. Even a multimillionaire would be taken aback by such a request.

"We'll see what can be done!"

Del Castillo did not give a definitive answer. I knew I just had to be patient and leave the rest up to God.

Fortunately, I did not have to wait long. Del Castillo sent me a most welcome email that same week: "Klaus, we'll give you the steel."

I leapt inwardly for joy and reread the email. I noticed he had addressed me by my first name, a sign of familiarity and rapport.

It has almost always been a personal relationship between myself and potential donors that has been the deciding factor in whether or not they choose to help Diospi Suyana. It is not what is in one's bank account but, rather, what is in one's heart that determines the desire to give. In my Spanish presentations, I usually spoke too fast and skipped over words, but despite my imperfect rhetoric I often saw tears in the eyes of my audience. Afterwards, many made decisions to give more generously than they had ever done in their lives before.

A director of Cayetano Heredia University once described the effect of my presentations as pure magic. I see it as the blessing of God. The Bible says that God directs people's hearts like streams of water. Remembering this removes a heavy burden from me. Success, even in the most difficult situations, is not dependent on me, but on God. There is nothing more important than faith in the Living God. He alone can make the "impossible" possible.

The legal department of MDH invited me to return to Lima to discuss the next steps. The attorney pointed out that Diospi Suyana would need to be registered with the tax authorities as a charity so that the substantial gift of MDH would be tax deductible. This official charity status had to be personally approved by the Peruvian Minister of Finance.

I did not lack imagination but had no idea how to pull off something like this.

The attorney gave me a strange look and said, "Dr. John, you are a man of faith. You will have it taken care of within a week."

I was not so sure, and left somewhat discouraged. The steel and the hospital roof were sliding from my grasp.

Since everything in South America runs on personal contacts, I went up to the next floor to say hello to Guido del Castillo. His office door was closed, but his secretary invited me to take a seat until he was available.

Whenever I am in Lima, I am always short of time. Now was no exception. I kept glancing at my watch; two more minutes and I would have to leave. Just at that moment, the office door opened and del Castillo appeared, smiling. He beckoned me in, and after the usual exchange of pleasantries I steered the conversation to the quandary I was facing.

"Señor Castillo, I will do what I can to get the signature of the Minister of Finance. I don't know how, but it will work out."

He looked over at me thoughtfully.

"Oh, Klaus," he mumbled, "that is all way too complicated."

On sudden impulse, he reached for the phone and ordered the full amount of steel for the roof. This decision meant that he would not be able to deduct his gift from his taxes.

Later, I had to smile. The attorney had predicted that I would get everything I needed within a week. It had taken all of fifteen minutes.

In November, three tractor trailers hauled fifty-five tons of steel profile up to Curahuasi, and the welders from Untecsa immediately started work on the intricate construction of the roof. Following a presentation before the Chamber of Miners on October 26, also arranged by del Castillo, I found myself before the Director of Marketing for Southern Peru. As a result, we were sent the asbestos-free roof tiles we needed: a donation worth about $50,000.

As I looked back on this series of gifts, I realized with amazement how it had all come about. We had just received goods valued at $120,000 from two Peruvian companies, because of a report in a weekly magazine, which in turn was the result of the public relations work by IMPSAT who had wanted to publicize the donation of a satellite dish. The satellite dish came about because I had lost my projector and was seeking to replace it through one company whose owner was related to the owner of the other. Back in December 2005 I had lost property worth $1,000, but by the end of 2007 I had gained nearly $200,000 in goods and services for Diospi Suyana.

It is this incredible journey with God that truly enriches our lives, not the accumulation of material wealth. Guido del Castillo set up four more interviews for me with mining trade journals. When Monica Belling published a one-page report about Diospi Suyana in her journal, *ProActivo*, nobody could have guessed where it would lead. The magazine had a circulation of only 5,000, but a copy landed in the hands of Renato Canales, the producer of *90 Segundos*, a news program on one of Peru's major TV networks. In March, he invited me to his office to share more about Diospi Suyana. Then things moved fast. He sent a film crew to Curahuasi, and in April the station broadcast three reports during peak viewing times, bringing the news of Diospi Suyana into the living rooms of millions of Peruvians.

Only God can turn defeat into victory. I do not mean that faith in God makes us rich in financial terms per se. This is no "prosperity gospel." But when we turn our lives over to Him, even painful setbacks serve a purpose and move us on towards a greater goal. This has been my experience, and I try to share it with every audience to whom I have the opportunity to speak.

36

Siege Conditions

Each month, the Constructec office in Quito would present us with an invoice for work done. Carlos Pullas and John Walter had always slapped an additional 20 per cent profit on top of the fixed costs. If Constructec had actually applied themselves fully to the work, we might have tolerated their questionable billing practices, but this was by no means the case. Daniel Lind, the young engineer who was supervising construction for Constructec in Curahuasi, seemed pretty cut off from and forgotten by the head office in Ecuador. Udo Klemenz and I became increasingly discontented with the company's practices, and the emails between Ecuador and Peru became increasingly harsh.

We had found out that Constructec had not put our initial advance payment of $100,000 to good use. They had paid excessive prices for some of the materials, enabling them to increase their own profit margin. Essentially, the more irresponsibly they spent our supporters' money, the more money they earned for themselves.

When we learned from Daniel Lind that the bank guarantee for our first payment to Constructec had expired without notice, I had finally had enough. Under the seal of secrecy, I made Daniel a very tempting offer.

"If you work for us, we will pay you considerably more –

172

and we'll all have Constructec off our backs!"

The crooked managers in Quito seemed to have guessed our plans and threatened to stop construction immediately. They accused us of not having enough money to guarantee continuation of construction. The fate of Diospi Suyana hung by a thread once again.

I had another German tour planned for November 2006. I learned that, two days after my scheduled departure, Constructec intended to stop building and to pursue legal action against us, thinking I would be powerless to intervene from so far away. The evening before I left, I sat in the living room with Tina and the children, feeling at the absolute end of my rope. In search of any glimmer of hope, I opened my Bible and read Psalm 31. Three thousand years ago, King David had uttered words that spoke assurance into my very situation. Verses 21 and 22 read: "Praise be to the Lord, for he showed me the wonders of his love when I was in a city under siege. In my alarm I said, 'I am cut off from your sight!' Yet you heard my cry for mercy when I called to you for help."

The freeze on construction never happened. Tough rounds of negotiation were held with Constructec until the end of the year. In one evening meeting, Carlos Pullas jumped up from the table in fury and traveled all the way back to Quito that same night.

The experience that Udo Klemenz brought to the table and support from Attorney Klaus Schultze-Rhondorf in Germany proved to be invaluable. On January 23, we signed a cancellation agreement, which permitted us to terminate our business relationship with Constructec following payment of an outstanding balance of $39,000, and without incurring the penalty that would normally be imposed in the event of an early termination of contract.

Our signatures on the document were barely dry when Udo Klemenz made another alarming discovery. Constructec had skimmed off an additional $34,000, allegedly to cover their taxes on their profit from Diospi Suyana. But criminal tendencies had made a tax evader out of Carlos Pullas, and so the Peruvian government had never seen the money. Meanwhile, he had fled the country, back to the safety of Quito. This criminal offense would make it impossible for us to claim back the tax we were entitled to as a non-profit organization. So we deducted the amount from the outstanding balance, and transferred only the remaining $5,000 to Constructec.

We had finally got rid of Carlos Pullas, John Walter, and their like. At least that is what we thought at the time. Daniel Lind now managed construction for Diospi Suyana as an independent contractor. As $2 million more was still needed to finish the hospital, we were thrilled to be saving the $400,000 that Constructec would have taken as extra profit.

God set Diospi Suyana free, just as He did "a city under siege." The increased financial latitude meant we could step up the pace of construction. We could continue our work with renewed energy and assurance.

37

The First Members of Staff Arrive

The success of the Diospi Suyana concept hinged on the audacious supposition that at least thirty doctors, nurses, and administrative specialists would be willing to move to Peru with us. We weren't talking about a short-term adventure or tour, but a commitment of years, full of uncertainty and risk. Anybody volunteering to give up their job in Germany, Switzerland, or Austria had to seriously weigh the adverse effects on their long-term career path as well as the drastic reduction in salary. It is relatively easy to support overseas work with a check, written in the comfort of one's own office. It is a far different matter to uproot one's family completely and settle in a foreign land far away from all that is loved and familiar. We were seeking people who would be willing to give up the comforts they had known thus far, and willing to step out in faith, raising their own support as missionaries. We needed men and women in the prime of life, as crazy as we were. For many, this was too great a sacrifice to ask.

Maybe one in 10,000 would consider doing something this drastic as an expression of their faith, and it was our task to seek out these rare individuals, wherever they might be.

Every media report served a double purpose: soliciting much-needed funds but also advertising critical Diospi Suyana staff vacancies. Whenever a doctor or nurse sent an email inquiry about the terms of employment, they were given our full attention. We would usually then organize an event in their hometown, sharing our presentation with their church, workplace, and friends.

On November 22, 2004, twenty-two highly motivated professionals attended the first official Diospi Suyana information session for potential staff members. Of the attendees of this historic meeting in Wiesbaden, twelve did actually "jump the Pond" over to Peru to work with us. We held these information sessions several times a year at various locations in Germany, sharing, encouraging, and dispelling concerns, but most of all emphasizing that Diospi Suyana was a work of faith and total dependence on God.

Not everyone who enthusiastically expressed interest in our mission was able to make a full commitment to see it through. But, as if guided by an invisible hand, the first staff members began to roll in. In November 2005, we welcomed Lyndal Maxwell, an Australian radiographer we had met at the Vozandes del Oriente Hospital. She became an integral part of our planning team and even translated our German project proposal into English. She very obviously had a heart for the work we were doing. Lyndal is a first-class pioneer; she is extremely adaptable and can find her niche just about anywhere, including a dirty mud hut. Her enthusiasm and her ability to work under pressure made her an indispensable member of our team.

In April 2006, we were joined by Gerhard and Heike Wieland, newly-weds who left Germany to join our nursing staff. We were greatly impressed by their flexibility and calm demeanor. No matter what they were asked to do, they consistently gave their best and never complained. Gerhard's standard response to any request was "No problem!"

In August, the Engelhard family arrived in Peru from Emden. Oliver and Birgit brought their three children, and initially had their hands full attempting to establish a comfortable home in rustic surroundings. Just like the rest of our new arrivals, the new life in South America began with several months of intensive study at the local language school.

Towards the end of 2006, we were joined by a contingent of five women who referred to themselves collectively as "Girl Power." Ortrun Heinz from the Charité Hospital in Berlin had already had the experience of setting up not one but two nursing schools in her career. Now, at sixty-five, she was thrilled to be bringing her wealth of knowledge to the emerging mission hospital. From Switzerland came nurse Cornelia Bühler, in absolute certainty that Curahuasi was where God wanted her to be, despite all the initial hardships. Dr. Renate Engisch, a radiologist, and two young women from Saxony completed the merry troupe. Nurse Marit Weilbach and radiographer Bettina Baumgarten actually belonged to the same church but had applied separately to be part of Diospi Suyana.

By the end of December 2006, we were up to fourteen staff members and six children in the Diospi Suyana "family."

All of these trailblazers needed to keep a positive focus so as not to crack under the pressure and adverse conditions. Here they were, far removed from everything they had known, dropped into an unfamiliar culture with an incomprehensible language. Their houses were made of mud, which back in Germany was the sort of shelter that would have been used for animals. Their future place of employment was only a shell of a building, and nobody could predict when it might be up and running. They each drew courage from their assurance that God had a special purpose for them here. As soon as they finished language school, they jumped into doing whatever was needed at Diospi Suyana.

Many got involved in the children's work that Tina and Lyndal had started in December 2005. They had created a kind of scouting program, with fifteen boys and girls attending at the outset. The popularity of the program soared, and it wasn't long before seventy children were regularly participating. Obviously, the increasing number of children required a larger meeting space than the living room that had been used, so the group moved outdoors in front of the house. A nearby school offered the use of their facilities, and as we accrued more volunteer assistance the Kids' Clubs expanded until nearly 300 boys and girls were coming.

In the Peruvian highlands, children are perhaps the most disenfranchised members of society. Even the youngest are sent out to do strenuous physical labor in the fields. Children are frequently neglected by their parents. Many families are burdened by poverty, alcoholism, and more mouths than they can possibly care for – it is basically not an environment conducive to raising healthy children. At the Kids' Clubs, children were provided with both loving care and opportunities for learning. As they did crafts, they learned how to use tools such as scissors. They learned how to do puzzles and simply enjoyed "being kids" with others their age. Most importantly, they learned that Jesus loves them, and that, in His eyes, they are all special – no matter how poor or sick they might be.

Although medicine has been our primary focus, our work with children has been a source of great blessing. The Kids'

Clubs are a critical investment in the future of the Quechua young people, who are likely to suffer much from increasing ethnic discrimination, global warming, and economic crises. With faith in God, they will learn to face life's challenges with courage.

38

The Christmas Gift from Siemens

E ven in so-called "Third-World" countries, patients with financial means can obtain medical treatment from private clinics which is of a standard comparable to care in Western hospitals. But for the majority of the population, particularly those living outside major metropolitan areas, there are only state-run medical centers of varying caliber available. The Peruvian "Postas de Salud" lack basics such as medication and motivated staff.

It was in precisely such a rural setting that we wanted to build a modern mission hospital that would allow the mountain population access to more advanced medicine. It was our dream for a more equitable world, and although it may have sounded strange to the audiences we spoke to over the years, we found that many shared this hope.

Although sophisticated technology such as computer axial tomography (CAT) was virtually unheard of in our remote location, we had planned to have a CAT scanner at Diospi Suyana. Such a device would provide valuable diagnostic information in a matter of minutes, potentially saving many lives. It was, however, extremely expensive.

On March 25, 2006, I gave my presentation at the guest house at Bremen University. The former mayor, Henning Scharf, and a team from the NDR television station were present. After the evening's program, we all relaxed together at the pub. The woman sitting next to me was an employee of Siemens. All that evening, she promised she would try to use her influence within the company to garner some support for Diospi Suyana. As it turned out, she was not actually able to help much, but she planted an idea in my head. I decided to put out feelers to see whether Siemens or Philips might be able to help us obtain the CAT scanner for our hospital.

Large companies are inundated with letters every month, all begging for this or that. Most of these end up in the garbage, unread. But I was stubborn by nature, a fact that often drove my wife up the wall. I wrote letter after letter and email after email. I called any number that seemed remotely promising and talked until I went hoarse. On September 5, I had the opportunity to speak in person at Philips. Before entering the Philips building, I called Siemens from the parking lot and asked for an appointment to discuss our urgent need of a CAT scanner. Half an hour later, I was making the same request of the Philips managers. Although I may indeed be stubborn, my relentless campaign for a CAT scanner had as yet met with no success, even after nine months of trying.

In December, Tina surprised me with the message that a Dr. Feldhaus had called from Siemens to offer us a CAT scanner at no charge. Now either Tina had misunderstood, a reasonable possibility given the quality of our phone connections, or Siemens had just announced a most astounding Christmas gift! Still, as we had nothing in writing, we kept our feet on the ground.

On February 9, 2007, I took the elevator up to the fourteenth floor of the Siemens headquarters in Erlangen. Dr. Feldhaus had invited me to lunch so that we could discuss the details of the phenomenal contribution.

He was a big man, respectable and very open to charitable causes, which was a surprise to me since Siemens had not previously done much to distinguish itself on the humanitarian front. On the contrary, it had just endured the worst corporate scandal in the company's history. It seemed that nearly every day there was another story in the paper about newly discovered bribes and other illegal dealings with interesting customers such as the Nigerian dictator, Abacha. The entire management structure of Siemens was very much on edge.

Dr. Feldhaus enjoyed the culinary delights of the Siemens dining room while my laptop and I shared the story of Diospi Suyana. My lunch partner was visibly moved.

"Dr. John, let me tell you why Siemens is going to give you a CAT scanner." Evidently, Dr. Feldhaus was about to let me in on a little secret. "By the way, this is the first time we have donated a CAT scanner to a South American hospital."

The story he shared as I started in on my lunch, now grown cold, sounded as if it had come right out of a novel. It is said that truth is stranger than fiction…

"I have been the Director of Communications at Siemens Medical Solutions since October of last year. I received your letter very soon after taking this position."

I chewed thoughtfully on my cauliflower and listened carefully.

"I was supposed to write you a letter of refusal," Dr. Feldhaus continued, "but when I read in your letter about your faith in God, I became unsettled. I too am a believer, a Catholic Christian, and I keep an open Bible on my desk."

I sipped at my water and hung on to every word. I really had not expected faith in God to be important to a Siemens official.

"I asked Professor Reinhard, President of Siemens Medical Solutions, if it would not be possible after all to give your hospital a CAT scanner, but he refused, saying it was against company policy to make such large donations."

I nodded imperceptibly. This sounded more like what I had expected.

"But you know, Dr. John, in December, Professor Reinhard himself authorized a charitable donation. The beneficiaries were doctors, just like you and your wife, and they were setting up a very similar medical project in Thailand. They were personal friends of Professor Reinhard, however, so he made an exception for them. When I found out about this, I again brought up your request for Diospi Suyana – and this time he agreed!"

The chronicle of this donation was almost unbelievable. It was more delicious than the dessert I was spooning into my mouth. Here we had a top-level manager acting on my behalf, even though he didn't know me. And on top of that, he had challenged the company rules – and the company president – because his faith in God was more important to him than his career.

The CAT scanner was duly donated and has been used hundreds of times at the mission hospital. Siemens informed its 400,000 employees worldwide of the extraordinary decision via the in-house magazine, *Siemens World*. Months later, Professor Reinhard became a casualty of his company's corrupt practices, and Dr. Feldhaus moved to Basel in the summer of 2010 to become a board member of the Roche company. In August 2007, he wrote me an email which will continue to bring joy to my heart for the rest of my days:

For me, Diospi Suyana is proof that God exists.

39

Packing Up

We had started back in the spring of 2004 with four sets of anesthetic equipment, and now, in September 2006, we had hundreds of donated items in storage at Schenck in Darmstadt. To be honest, it was a jumbled mix of modern, high-tech apparatus and machines of antediluvian appearance, a mish-mash of individual pieces. Some items bore witness to the generosity of the donors; others suggested that Diospi Suyana might have been misused as a cheap disposal route.

Regardless of where the equipment had come from or what sort of shape it was in, all of it, sooner or later, would need to be packed up and shipped to Peru. I knew from Mr. Weg that Schenck had its own packing department. Would it be worth asking for help there? I was told that Mr. Jürgen Theilmann, the assistant manager, would be my point of contact.

A little while later I sat in his office, hoping he would have some time to see me. As the minutes passed, I chatted with his friendly secretary, but unfortunately Mr. Theilmann remained unavailable and I had to go back to Wiesbaden without having accomplished anything.

Perhaps I had said a bit too much to the charming lady, because when I called Mr. Theilmann a few days later, he responded with unveiled irritation.

"My secretary has already told me about your request, Dr. John. You are really pushing it. Do you know how much packing material costs?"

"I have no idea," I answered meekly. "I'd just like to show you a few pictures on my laptop so that you understand why I am asking for your help."

I felt forced onto the defensive and was careful how I formulated my response.

"That will not be necessary," he fired back at me. "I know exactly what you want. Do you realize that we have already waived over $35,000 in storage costs for you?"

Mr. Theilmann's nose was clearly out of joint, but I had nothing to lose, so I kept pushing.

"Mr. Theilmann, please, just give me twenty minutes. You just have to see my short presentation."

"You can show me your presentation as many times as you want: it will do nothing to change the situation."

I took his flippant response as half an invitation. "Great! When can I come?"

"Hmm." Mr. Theilmann did not answer right away. "Be in my office at 8 a.m. the day after tomorrow, if you like."

Our conversation had just taken the best possible turn, and my silent prayer of thanks was more than justified.

I sensed there was a chance. Then I hit a massive traffic jam right outside Darmstadt. It was my philosophy that, if I am asking someone for something, the very least I can do in return is be on time. But the crazy situation on the roads was completely beyond my control. I dashed into Theilmann's office fifteen minutes late. What a blessing – he hadn't arrived himself yet! I sank into a comfortable chair and my pulse slowly returned to normal.

A few minutes later, the door opened and Mr. Theilmann rushed in.

"Dr. John – so sorry to keep you waiting. I was stuck in traffic." There was no sign of the grumpiness of our previous meeting. "What can I offer you to drink?"

The glass of water did me good. I opened up my laptop and launched into the story of Diospi Suyana. As always, I wanted to tell the *whole* story, and found it difficult to stick to the abbreviated version. After thirty minutes, I had sprinted through 220 pictures and was literally catching my breath. Mr. Theilmann appeared to be contemplating something.

"Tell me, Dr. John, can private individuals be part of your project?"

I nodded eagerly. "Of course! Many people are."

Wasn't that what I had been telling him for the past half hour, how countless people of all ages were advancing the Diospi Suyana dream with us?

"Then give me one of the sign-up forms. I want to provide support on a regular basis."

Before my eyes, a "Saul" was transformed into a "Paul." My critic of just forty-eight hours ago had joined the growing ranks of Diospi Suyana supporters.

We still hadn't touched on the subject at hand: the packaging of our equipment for overseas shipping. With a hint of daring optimism, Mr. Theilmann turned around and announced, "As far as packing and shipping goes, we have to find a solution. I will talk to my colleagues."

Not everyone who, in the heat of the moment, enthusiastically expresses a desire to support Diospi Suyana actually follows through with such a commitment. Perhaps they didn't have a pen to fill out the pledge card. Maybe they just hadn't found the time to set up a bank transfer. Or maybe they simply forgot. But Mr. Theilmann was a man of his word, and he has shown himself to be one of our most faithful supporters since that remarkable first meeting. He collaborated with Managing Director Karl-Heinz Pfuhl and Chief of Logistics Richard Heysel, as well as many other staff, in order to pull off an organized, highly professional packing project, a massive undertaking that dragged out over weeks. Throughout the spring and summer, company employees managed to load our motley collection of hospital equipment into nine large freight containers. They worked with such dedication and care that one might assume Diospi Suyana was paying them a fortune for their services. But there was no such compensation. In fact, Schenck itself assumed responsibility for all costs, right down to the last penny.

As the *Darmstädter Echo* reported on April 13, Schenck donated more than $60,000 in packing materials and labor. When you add in the storage fees waived over the last months, the total value of goods and services given to Diospi Suyana was well over $150,000. The generosity of Schenck did not stop there: since 2006, they have sent a substantial financial gift to Diospi Suyana each Christmas.

In November 2007, I was to return to the Schenck compound one last time. The Diospi Suyana crates had long since left storage. My purpose on this visit was simply to express my gratitude for all that the company had done for us. At a meeting of seventy staff members, I relayed the story of Diospi Suyana and highlighted Schenck's vital role.

When I had finished, Mr. Pfuhl grabbed the microphone and said a few words that I will always remember.

"When Dr. John asked us for help in the summer of 2005, our business was not doing very well. Today it is thriving, and we actually have more work than we can manage. It seems that a special blessing was given to us because of Diospi Suyana."

40

Seven Containers in One Fell Swoop

We had roughly estimated that we would need four containers to transport the equipment in storage at Schenck across the Atlantic. I was secretly hoping that the Streck Freight Company of Southern Germany would help us again. They had taken care of our first container in an exemplary manner, so why not repeat the good deed on a larger scale?

However, my inquiries in Lörrach failed to achieve success. One of the logistics managers made it quite clear that his company had more than met its quota for humanitarian action by transporting our repair-shop supplies from Kaltenbach. He suggested I contact the Hamburg Süd Shipping Company, and wished me luck.

I soon found their phone number via the company website, and without any inhibitions whatsoever I asked to be put through to the managing director's secretary. Like any good managing director's secretary, Ms. Matthiesen queried the nature of my business.

I waited several days for an answer, but received none. My impatience getting the better of me, I called again.

"Ms. Matthiesen," I pleaded, "I would happily drive for

ten hours to Hamburg and back if you could just get me ten minutes with the managing director."

She had probably never heard such an imploring entreaty before. I knew how odd I must have sounded, but my determination got her attention.

"Dr. John, please wait a little longer. I will discuss your case with the management."

That afternoon she called back with the fantastic news I would immediately post on the Diospi Suyana website: "Hamburg Süd approves shipment of four containers at no charge!" So there had been no need to drive to Hamburg after all.

I thanked Ms. Matthiesen profusely, and in my mind I could already see our precious cargo sailing smoothly on the high seas towards South America. But things don't always work out the way we expect, do they...

The packing could not be completed as planned before the end of the year because Schenck was working at capacity just to fill its Christmas orders.

I arrived back in Germany in February 2007, and walked round the storage rooms at Schenck. Looking at all the crates, it suddenly hit me: the donations had multiplied in my eight-week absence. There was no way all of this would fit into four containers. My fears were confirmed by the Chief of Logistics. Mr. Heysel, through very precise calculations, concluded we would need not four but *eight* containers! Alarms started going off in my head.

Another call to Hamburg would not be enough. I would have to go up there myself – and soon. I drove the 350 miles north in a rented car on a gray, drizzly, February day. A Mr. Gedde had agreed to see me for thirty minutes that afternoon. I found a parking space in the center of town and arrived on time, laptop in hand.

Mr. Gedde was a tall man, quiet but friendly. He followed my presentation with interest and did not flinch when I got down to my reason for coming.

"Mr. Gedde, you're not going to believe this, but instead of four containers, we are actually going to need eight."

He must have heard worse things in his life, because, without missing a beat, he replied, "Dr. John, you can have them."

He then patted me on the back and sent me back out into the Hamburg rain.

What a triumph! Double the number of containers meant that Diospi Suyana had been saved yet another $15,000 in charges. Not a bad outcome for ten hours on the highway!

In February, seven containers left Darmstadt on their long journey to Peru. DHL paid for the transportation within Germany, and then Hamburg Süd picked up the sea freight costs. In addition to the initial seven containers, the shipping company agreed to pay for another four. When, after shipping a total of eleven containers at no charge, they could no longer afford to help us in this manner, options opened up unexpectedly with other companies. An invisible hand guided me step by step, always in the right direction at the right time. All I had to do was seize each opportunity and not let go.

On April 16–18, the Peruvian television network "Frecuencia Latina" broadcast three reports about Diospi Suyana. As the third part was aired, the Hamburg Süd ship carrying the Diospi Suyana cargo made its way into the port of Callao. Two days later, I had an appointment with Ms. Gloria Luque, Director of Customs for Sea Freight. I gave her a CD containing the three news reports, and relayed a personal greeting from producer Renato Canales, as he had asked me to, winking as he did so. Ms. Luque got the message immediately.

"Oh, Dr. John, don't worry about your containers. They are practically through Customs!"

And indeed they were.

Within two hours, the Customs officials had waved seven large containers with $1.1 million worth of medical equipment straight through. Eighty pages full of small print detailing the contents of the containers were signed and stamped because of a single political decision.

At 7 p.m., I hand-delivered pizza to *Prosoi*, the Customs agency. The four agents and I had every reason to celebrate.

"Dr. John, we have been in the Customs business for seven years and we have never seen anything like this before!" agent Carmen Rosa exclaimed as she bit into her pizza.

April 23, 2007 saw the arrival of seven containers for the hospital. Almost all of our transport needs in Peru were taken care of by Neptunia.

The Kaltenbach Co. donated the hospital workshop.

Olaf Böttger, Chairman of Diospi Suyana, congratulates our 250th supporting member.

Thirty TV reports made Diospi Suyana famous throughout Peru as the "hospital of faith."

A stand in Lörrach. Innumerable fund-raising campaigns by clubs, churches, and private individuals raised a total of $14.5 million.

Dr. Sybille Storz donated equipment for laparoscopic surgery, as did their competitors Schölly. I visited 200 companies, most of which helped us with donations.

My wife and I had an audience with the First Lady of Germany Eva Luise Köhler in Bellevue Palace on March 20, 2007.

The Peruvian President's wife, Pilar Nores de García, with CAT scanner from Siemens.

The inauguration (from l. to r.): the President of Apurímac, David Salazar; the Peruvian Health Minister, Dr. Carlos Vallejos; the First Lady of Peru, Sra. Pilar Nores de García; my wife and I; Mr. Lamle from the German Embassy; and the General Consul Maria Jürgens.

View of the stage: the event was filmed by nine TV teams.

The First Lady of Peru cuts the red ribbon.

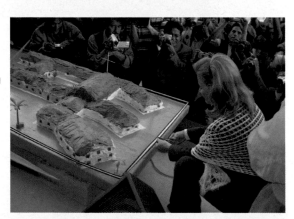

Below: My speech at the dedication in front of 4,500 people.

Above: 450 square feet of stained-glass windows, made up of 3,000 individual pieces.

Left: Volunteers sing a song at the dedication.

Bottom: An emergency generator from Detroit Diesel MTU.

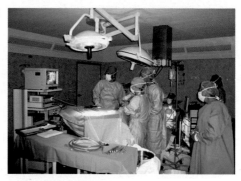

Top: The Diospi Suyana Hospital seen from the front.

Right: Dr. Jens Hassfeld carries out laparoscopic surgery.

A generous donation from Dräger is presented in person by Mrs. Claudia Dräger.

Left: People throng to the main entrance. Patients come from all over southern Peru.

Below: Audience on April 28, 2008 in the Presidential Palace.
(From r. to l.) Dr. David Brady, my wife and I, President Alan García and his wife, Pilar Nores, Dr. Victor Correa.

The Johns on June 4, 2006 on our local mountain in Curahuasi. There was not much to be seen yet on the construction site down in the valley. But we were firm in our faith.

And who said that faith in God was boring? Not us, for sure! October 22, 2009

41

Bellevue Palace

"Why do you want to speak to the Health Minister?"

Pastor Dario Lopez and Dr. Victor Arroyo frowned. Both the President and the Director of the Council of Evangelical Churches were expressing their apprehension.

"The government will only put up roadblocks for your hospital. It's best to leave well enough alone."

I ignored their counsel back in January 2003. A week later, I did meet the Peruvian Minister of Health, Dr. Carbone Campoverde, a devout Catholic and member of Opus Dei. Over the years, I have conferred with a total of nine Peruvian cabinet members. I believe that a project as large and potentially influential as Diospi Suyana should have at least the silent sanctioning of the political elite. I was not looking to further a political agenda, but I felt that the faith message of Diospi Suyana should be heard in all sectors of society.

I am always happy to read anything in the press that sheds a positive light on our Christian foundations. Every TV report that portrays Diospi Suyana as a work of faith is a source of great pleasure. The message of Christ crucified must not only be preached in our fallen world, it must be lived out. In Germany, a person's faith is considered a private matter, not to be shared in public. Anyone openly professing personal beliefs is usually subject to social disapproval, if not outright opposition. But demonstrating respect and tolerance for other beliefs does not mean I have to hide my own light under a bushel.

On January 25, 2007, I knocked at the door leading to the right-hand wing of the Presidential Palace, where, behind thick stone walls, lay the office of the First Lady of Peru. It was late, but Pilar Nores took half an hour to meet me. I had two important subjects to discuss. The first was the date of the hospital dedication: it was very important to me that she be able to attend. The other was a request for assistance with a particularly challenging matter: I wanted to try to get an audience with Eva Köhler, wife of the German President. Pilar Nores promised to help me, but we both knew the prospects of success were limited.

On February 19, I was sitting in a comfortable armchair at the home of the Peruvian Ambassador to Germany in Berlin. Professor Kaufmann-Doig had also offered his assistance when he had heard of my plans. Emails went back and forth between the Embassy in Germany and the Presidential Palace in Lima. The culmination was a two-page letter written by the Ambassador himself on behalf of Pilar Nores to the German Presidential Office, requesting an audience for my wife and me with the German First Lady.

I usually like to have more than one iron in the fire, so I also contacted the Nikel family, with whom I had been friends for years. Regine, a native of France, was always on the lookout for ways in which she could help us. Her husband, Rolf, is a high-ranking diplomat, very familiar with the inner workings of government power structures. In April 2004, when he was third in command at the German Embassy in Washington, he had gone way out on a limb for us. He had given Olaf Böttger and me an opportunity to address thirty embassy staff members at a gathering in his villa. Now, two and a half years later, he was working in Berlin, where he held an influential position in the Federal Chancellor's Office. At my request, Rolf contacted the German Presidential Office, seeking an audience for us with the First Lady. The response was not encouraging. It seemed that Mrs. Köhler was extremely popular, and inundated with requests for meetings. Very few of these requests could be granted. Even the official request from the Peruvian Embassy was not enough to open these doors.

Throughout February and March, I drove from one state to another, sharing my presentation at least thirty times, and stopping at my Wiesbaden apartment only briefly to change clothes or try to grab a few hours of sleep. I received some information from Rolf that encouraged me to be more creative in petitioning for an audience with the German First Lady. I discussed the situation by email and phone with the office of the Peruvian First Lady, and before the week was out Pilar Nores had written a personal letter to Mrs. Köhler on our behalf. This could help us immensely.

Standing in the shower on the morning of February 28, I suddenly had another idea. Why not ask Professor Ludwig Braun, Germany's most prominent industrialist, for a letter of recommendation? After all, he had given us ninety minutes of his precious time two years earlier.

Before taking off for an appointment in southern Germany, I called his office and followed up with an email. Just before midnight, I arrived back home to see the message light blinking on my answering machine. My exhaustion evaporated quickly as I recognized the voice of Mr. Braun, telling me he had personally put in a good word for us with Mrs. Köhler's office.

But, despite all the efforts in Lima, Melsungen, and

Berlin, we still had no idea whether or not Mrs. Köhler would ultimately agree to see us. Martin Luther once said that we should pray as if all our work were nothing, and work as if all our praying were in vain. I took this to heart as I drove from one end of Germany to the other, asking God for nothing less than an open door to Bellevue Palace.

On March 5, Cecilia Garrett from the Peruvian Embassy wrote to me, saying, "God and all our efforts have borne fruit. It is simply wonderful. It is my pleasure to inform you that you have an audience with Mrs. Köhler on March 20 at 1 p.m."

This news led to a flurry of phone calls. I would have to extend my stay in Germany by ten days. Tina and the children would come over from Peru for this momentous occasion. They would need plane tickets, and at very short notice.

The meeting with the First Lady was both a great honor and a tremendous opportunity, so I wanted to make the most of it. I called the Philips headquarters in Hamburg. The year before, I had given our presentation to two of the directors, but after months of deliberation the company had ultimately decided not to contribute anything to our efforts in Peru. Now, in view of our upcoming audience with Mrs. Köhler, Philips had a change of heart, donating a brand-new ultrasound machine with two transducers – a gift worth about $35,000.

At 1 a.m. on March 20, Tina and I crawled out of our car and into the cold beds of a motel just south of Berlin. There was no way we could really relax, but sleep overtook us just the same.

Our visit to the Presidential Office had been organized with military precision. At 12.45 p.m., we entered the official residence of the Federal President via a side entrance. A woman escorted us to a quintessential palace hall on the second floor. The heavy chandelier hanging from the ceiling, the luxurious deep-pile carpet on the floor, and the elegantly upholstered furniture composed a very distinguished setting for our talks. Queen Luise of Prussia looked down on us from an oil painting on the wall.

We positioned our laptop behind an armchair and opened the PowerPoint file. I had expressed my desire for this meeting to Pilar Nores in Lima back in January. Almost two months had passed since then, and now here we were, Tina and I, our hearts racing. In awe and anticipation, we stared at the heavy wooden door through which Mrs. Köhler and her advisors would enter at precisely 1 o'clock.

The forty-five-minutes allotted for our presentation flew by, but it was sufficient opportunity to communicate our dream to the First Lady of Germany. The atmosphere was receptive, and our appointment ended with a group photo.

It was like a fairy tale. In the fall of 2003, our entire family was sleeping on mattresses on the floor of a mud house. Three and a half years later, the wife of the German President was applauding our humanitarian work in Peru. Against all odds, we had developed this vision in the name of Christian love, and now it was being acknowledged by such high authority.

42

Such Expensive Church Windows?

A cab ride across Lima really is no picnic, especially at 5 o'clock in the afternoon.

"San Marcos University, please," I told the driver, and negotiated the price to be on the safe side.

As he pulled out into the throng of traffic, the houses seemed barely to creep by. A snail would have made better progress.

On the left, the Maria Reina Catholic Church came into view, and its stained-glass windows caught my eye. The builders had just completed the shell of our own hospital chapel, and it was now time to do the windows.

"If only I could talk to the priest about the stained glass," I thought.

My cab rolled along another hundred yards.

The driver suddenly turned round and said to me, "Señor, I'm afraid I cannot take you downtown – I have another customer at six."

He must have been astonished when I jumped out of the cab with a beaming smile.

Two minutes later I entered the church office, where various people were engaged in different jobs.

"Can someone please tell me about your beautiful stained-glass windows?" I asked.

A man stood up and came over to me.

"I'm glad you like them!"

"Yes, they are fantastic," I replied. "Who made them?"

I learned they were made by a German artist in the 1980s, and that the artist had since passed on. I took a few photos of the windows and drove back to the guest house in Lima, having cancelled my appointment at the university.

In the evening I checked my email. As usual, I seemed to have about fifty new messages. As I skimmed through them, I discovered an interesting piece of information from Udo Klemenz. Without being asked, he had sent me the exact dimensions of the chapel windows.

The next morning I was sitting at the computer, deliberating over what to post for the daily update on the Diospi Suyana website. It suddenly hit me: I would focus on the chapel windows. Nobody knew yet what they would look like, but I would write about them.

I was just beginning to compose my short report when Dirk Pograntz, a teacher at the Evangelical Seminary in Lima, came into the room with his wife. They were in the process of looking for a new place to live. When they saw the photos of the Maria Reina Church on my computer, they remarked, "We saw windows just like that in a home we viewed yesterday."

What absolutely perfect timing! They pulled the newspaper with the property listing out of their bag and gave me the landlord's telephone number.

The woman who answered the phone was very helpful. She told me that the artist who had made the windows was German and had died a number of years ago. The story sounded familiar. She no doubt meant the same man who had designed the church windows.

"I know an architect who is very familiar with leaded windows," she continued, giving me an unexpected lead.

Fortunately, she had the phone number handy, so I made my next call.

On Saturday afternoon, Jorge Rati welcomed me to his villa. The sculptures in his garden and the expensive wooden furniture were evidence of a refined, sophisticated taste. I shared my presentation once again, and it made a deep impression.

"Yes, I can help you," Mr. Rati said graciously. "I know pretty much everybody in Lima in this line of business."

Four days later, architect Alexandro Gallo, his wife, Gina de Bernardy, and her friend all heard the story of Diospi Suyana. Like Jorge, they were of Italian origin and knew a great deal about the art of leaded glass.

"Dr. John, we would be glad to draw up the drafts, and we are willing to do so at no charge. However, you will need to find the stained glass."

Mr. Gallo was a realist through and through, and did not mince words as he cautioned, "Leaded-glass panes are insanely expensive, and they cost even more in Peru than they do in Europe."

I mumbled something about glass being donated in the future, and thanked them politely for their time.

A few weeks later, I was back in Germany with a to-do list that included the item "stained glass." I wanted to find out more about it and hoped to begin organizing donations for our chapel windows.

On Saturday, June 9, I met an old friend, Andreas Koch, in Wiesbaden-Nordenstadt. He owns a printing business, and he and his brother, Matthias, sponsor the printing of the Diospi Suyana newsletter.

"Say, Andreas," I asked thoughtfully, "do you know anyone who works for Schott Glassworks?"

"Sure! Three Schott employees are members of our church."

Andreas' quick answer was a welcome surprise. While I tested how fast I could spin around on the office swivel chair (joy does strange things to people!), Andreas placed a call to a friend and gave him the scoop.

Monday brought discouraging news: Schott had transferred mass production of stained glass to Malaysia. Their subsidiary office in Grünenplan, in Lower Saxony, was the only place in Germany where any stained glass was being produced, and only in small amounts. I went ahead and rang them. The head of the Grünenplan office, Mr. Albrecht, was away, but his secretary encouraged me to make my request in writing. I mailed my letter that same afternoon.

I was staying in Germany for only two weeks this time, and my schedule was already packed with presentations in six different states and a trip to the Roche corporate office in Switzerland. On Friday, June 15, I received a response from Schott, declining to fulfill my request. Their official policy was not to donate any glass, so I had got my hopes up for nothing. As a consolation, though, they were going to send me two crates of samples – fifty panes, each twelve inches long.

As odd as it may sound, rather than defeating me, bad news sometimes gives me inspiration for further action. I got on the phone and soon had a Mr. Hofrichter on the line. He is the manager of the Derix Glass Studios in Wiesbaden-Wehen, an establishment that produces stained glass.

"Dr. John," he explained, "you will need the lead profiles as well, not just the stained-glass panes."

"Hmm," I cleared my throat, trying to hide my ignorance.

He told me that, in Germany, Jansen & Buscher in Krefeld had a virtual monopoly on lead-profile production. Mr. Hofrichter and I arranged to meet in his office the following Monday. When I hung up the phone, I immediately called Jansen & Buscher.

Companies are sometimes like medieval fortresses. As you approach them with a request, the secretary pulls up the drawbridge and you land in the moat. One such humiliating, futile, and *cold* dunking is often enough to discourage further attempts. But this time, I was in luck. The secretary put me straight through to a Mr. Kröger, who listened attentively to an abbreviated version of the Diospi Suyana story.

"Dr. John," he finally said, "send me an email. The board is meeting tomorrow and we will discuss your request."

What miraculous timing! Full of enthusiasm, I formulated a polite petition and launched it into cyberspace. No sooner was the weekend over than I called Mr. Kröger back.

"May I ask what the board decided?"

"In your favor! We will donate the profiles. We just need to know the exact quantity you need."

At that moment, I could visualize the lead framework for our chapel windows. There was no glass yet, but all the same…

Mr. Kröger was just about to hang up when I blurted out, "By the way, our container is being packed this Saturday, four days from now. It would be great if your profiles could go with this shipment."

Now I really had gone too far.

Mr. Kröger spluttered, "What are you thinking? We have to send your order to the Production Department. It will be two weeks before we can deliver – at least. And you don't even know how much you need!"

I sighed. "If it can't be done, it can't be done," I conceded softly and hung up the receiver.

I then called the Schott-Grünenplan office, as I knew Mr. Albrecht would be back from his business trip. Within seconds, I had the right man on the phone.

"Thank you for the samples, Mr. Albrecht," I said. "Could I maybe come by and show you some pictures of our work in Peru?"

Mr. Albrecht sounded very friendly, but refused politely. "We are not allowed to donate any glass. I am very sorry, but it would be a waste of your time."

"On Thursday, I will be in Lemgo, which isn't too far from you. I would be happy to stop by in the morning."

With this logic, Mr. Albrecht was willing for me to come.

In the afternoon, I visited Mr. Hofrichter at Derix. As I walked into the studio, my eyes grew wide as I saw tables full of talented hands arranging stained-glass fragments into impressive mosaics. These were clearly experts at work, and I knew it would be wise not to reveal my complete lack of familiarity with their art. After my presentation, Mr. Hofrichter calculated the amount of lead profile we would need, and I passed that information on to Mr. Kröger that evening.

On Wednesday, I drove to Lower Saxony, arriving in Grünenplan about 1.30 a.m. Despite my late arrival, I was still on time for my Thursday-morning meeting with Mr. Albrecht and his colleague, who followed my presentation with great interest.

When I was done, Mr. Albrecht asked, "Dr. John, does your car have a large trunk?"

I nodded vigorously in response.

"Alright then, let's fill it!" he instructed.

For a whole hour, Mr. Albrecht himself selected the prettiest pieces of glass for me and wrapped them in thick packaging paper.

My rental car rode conspicuously low as I drove back to Wiesbaden the next day. I had a miracle in my trunk, and now I was listening to a second miracle on the phone: Mr. Kröger of Jansen & Buscher could not explain how it was possible, but our lead profiles had already been sent to our storage site in Darmstadt, cutting the delivery time from the projected two weeks to a mere four days.

That was incredible news! At the very last moment, I had got all the materials I needed for the stained-glass windows: the lead profiles from Krefeld, and the fifty sample panes plus my trunk full of glass from Grünenplan. I simply had to tell this wonderful story to the head of the studio at Derix.

"Mr. Hofrichter," I asked, "could you possibly give us two crates of glass as well – to top things off?"

Who could turn me down after hearing of such fantastic developments? Not Mr. Hofrichter.

"Come by later. I'll have everything ready!"

In August 2007, Alexandro Gallo drove from Lima to Curahuasi to take a look at the glass. He checked into a local hotel, where he spent several days painstakingly designing the twenty chapel windows. He would not accept a single dollar for his creative work, but did request that we purchase some cheaper Peruvian glass to complete his brilliant designs.

It took four master artisans from the capital an entire month to put the thousands of glass pieces together like a giant puzzle, an arduous task for which they would accept only half of their usual remuneration. The total 450 square feet of stained glass ended up costing us $6,000, including labor and material. In Europe, the price would have easily been 100 times that amount. Visitors from Europe often shake their heads in disapproval when they see the windows. They wonder how on earth Diospi Suyana could justify spending so much donor money on *art*, rightly estimating that the value of the windows was well over half a million dollars. But we didn't pay that bill, nor did our financial supporters – God Himself did.

When the sun's rays pour through the colored glass panes, they cast the most glorious reflections on the white walls opposite. During our morning devotions, 150 staff members and patients sit in the chapel, full of awe. Although they are poor, the resplendent beauty causes them to look past their present circumstances, as if through a window into heaven.

43

A Bold Troupe

In the six months leading up to the hospital's dedication, the number of committed staff members swelled to thirty-three. Anyone thinking that these highly motivated professionals were looking to "escape" something back home or lacked the ability to compete in a developed country's medical field would be sorely wrong. Dubbing them either "adventurers" or "idealists" would also be a bit of a misnomer, for while our newly arrived volunteers certainly did bring a sense of idealism, curiosity, and a willingness to take risks, there was so much more calling them to serve in Peru. They had all come from different church backgrounds; nevertheless, they shared the same conviction that faith in God should manifest itself in more than pious platitudes. It should spur us on to action, for the good of our brothers and sisters, and to the glory of God. This group was ready to roll up their sleeves and get started.

I had met them all over the last five years. Tina and I had talked at length with each of them. Without exception, they had caught our enthusiasm upon seeing the Diospi Suyana presentation. My own motivation in striving for the success of this project had much to do with an intense desire to grow closer to God. My gaze was always on the distant horizon of eternity, and I was always hopeful of seeing the reality of God in the present. Many called to the mission field share this perspective.

We never tried to pressure or cajole anyone into going to Peru. On the contrary, we were bluntly honest about the challenges of this venture. There were dangers in the Peruvian highlands, and many disappointments would inevitably come. We all struggled with culture shock and learning a new language. But, for as often as I pointed all this out during our regular meetings for potential staff members, there were those thirty-three who either didn't listen or whose resolution to come could not be deterred. They had given up their apartments, handed in their notice at work, and said goodbye to their parents.

At the end of January 2007, nurse Carolin Müller of Ilmenau packed her bags. She had previous experience of humanitarian outreach, serving alongside her father, a physician of the highest caliber. She wanted to take a leading role in setting up the Diospi Suyana surgical department.

Timo and Simone Klingelhöfer stepped off the plane in Lima in March. As an electrician and information technology specialist, his role would naturally be to set up and maintain both our computer and our security systems. His wife, Simone, was a physical therapist and looked forward to helping future patients grow stronger.

In the first week of May, a group of three made the trip to Peru together. There was Stefan Höfer, who would be setting up our ICU. His wife, Petra, was an experienced radiographer and lab technician. And then there was Hanna Böker, who, at fifty-seven, was making a drastic career change in order to run the hospital's administration department. A former director of Fresenius, Inc., who had known Hanna for years, could not make sense of what she was doing at all. He told me in confidence that she was the best tax expert he had ever

I HAVE SEEN GOD

known. He simply couldn't fathom how she could walk away from such a successful career.

The next week, the Jochum family arrived. Burkhart, a master carpenter, had set a very ambitious goal for himself of crafting all of the doors and most of the closets for the hospital within a year. He implemented his plan with impressive fervor, later describing his time in Peru as the most precious year of his life. His wife, Carolin, a native Peruvian from Cusco, helped with translation and with the Kids' Clubs. As soon as they arrived in Lima, they and their three children all donned bright red T-shirts which boldly proclaimed "I LOVE PERU!"

In mid-August it was like a mass migration, as Michael and Elisabeth Mörl and their four children arrived from Saxony, bringing with them Frederike Simmchen, who would assist in schooling the children. Michael had worked for many years at the Dresden Cardiology Clinic ICU, but his practical gifts drew him more and more into the field of materials engineering and equipment repair. On top of all that he is a trained miller, and felt obliged to supply us with German bread.

Elisabeth is a licensed dietician and was soon turning heads at the local market where she bought large quantities of fruit and vegetables to ensure that her family had a healthy diet.

The Mörls were joined by Tove Hohaus from Meiningen. This young anesthesiologist had dreamed of serving as a missionary since her teenage years, but admittedly felt somewhat deflated on seeing the old anesthetic equipment stored in Darmstadt.

Katrin Krägler, a young woman from the executive department of a hospital, had found a Diospi Suyana flyer in her mailbox one day. Reading it had set her life on a completely different course.

Gynecologist Jens Hassfeld and his wife, Damaris, had read about our project in the August 2004 edition of *Family*. They set out for Peru with their four children, leaving behind grandparents and one unhappy boss.

The Bardys and the Bradys arrived at the end of August, and it was quite a while before ordinary mortals could get their almost identical names straight. Dr. David Brady was Diospi Suyana's answer to the urological problems of southern Peru. Pediatrician Dr. Dorothea Brady was responsible for our smallest patients, and cared for her own two children as well. She had spent part of her childhood in turbulent South Africa and subsequently possessed an indomitable spirit. She supported her husband completely when we asked that he take on the additional duties of assistant director of the hospital.

Birgit Bardy from Lüdenscheid was qualified both in internal medicine and as a general practitioner. She was fluent in Spanish, having lived in Spain as a child. She and her husband, Jörg, a physical therapist, had made a decision for life: they came to Peru with no plans to leave.

The team was characterized by many strong personalities. They may not have known exactly what was awaiting them, but they had a very clear sense of what they wanted to achieve. They were all brilliant, highly qualified professionals. Leading them was going to be an exciting, if not always easy, task for Tina and me.

44

Panic, Prayer, and Progress

Only 300 more yards to the front door! I had been traveling around Lima by cab all day, giving presentations to three different companies. Completely worn out, I dragged myself down the dark street to the guest house in Surco, southern Lima, fit only for my bed. All of a sudden, the ground under my feet began to shake violently. A strange noise seemed to rise from the depths to the earth's surface. The power poles started to sway and there were sharp hissing sounds as the cables touched and short-circuited.

I stood still in the middle of the street. The quake lasted over two minutes and registered 7.1 on the Richter scale, as the news reporters would announce later. I glanced at my watch; it was just before 7 p.m.

The earthquake on Wednesday, August 15 caused the breakdown of all telephone and email communication. The 8 million inhabitants of Lima crowded around TV screens, waiting for an official statement from the government. In the northern part of the capital several walls had collapsed, but there was no major damage. It seemed the city had been largely spared, as the epicenter was a good five hours' drive away to the south, near Pisco.

Two hours went by, and there was no news from the crisis zone. The entire country almost literally held its breath, desperately hoping and praying, but dreading the very worst. President Alan García attempted to calm the Peruvian people, initially reporting a total of nineteen dead, with the situation expected to be under control very shortly. As the night went on, the first of the terrible reports flashed around the world: this monstrous catastrophe had flattened entire communities, and the number of dead or missing was rising by the hour.

The extent of the tragedy became heartbreakingly apparent as the sun rose the next morning. People's faces contorted in horror as growing piles of bodies were captured by TV cameras. The rescue teams fought desperately against the clock in the hope of finding any remaining survivors buried in the rubble.

With Peru turned upside down by this cruel act of nature, it was difficult to think about anything other than the suffering of its people, caught in the throes. And yet time wasn't stopping for anyone.

A few months earlier, I had set a date for the dedication of the mission hospital, a ceremony in which First Lady Pilar Nores de García was to play a critical role. This date, August 31, was only a few days away. How in the world could this now happen, with the whole country still reeling from the tragic blow of a major earthquake?

On Monday morning, August 19, death and destruction still saturated all television and newspaper reports. Udo Klemenz, Daniel Lind, and I sat together in the office. If, by some miracle, the hospital could open on schedule after what had just happened, we had exactly twelve days to pull it together. Large parts of the hospital were still very obviously unfinished. We did have over 100 workers on site, but what could they do when our bank accounts had dwindled past the point of actually being able to pay for anything? A query regarding our dollar account revealed a total balance of $58. In our Peruvian currency account, we had a grand total of 23 soles, equivalent to about $7.

"Udo, there is no point in planning further," I said in resignation. "We simply have no money."

If the First Lady of Peru, the Minister of Health, and the media were to come to Curahuasi at the end of August, it would be nothing short of humiliating. Udo nodded despondently. We were, for all practical purposes, completely immobilized.

"Udo, let's pray."

Udo shrugged his shoulders. Prayer was the wisest, if not the only, thing we could do in this situation. We closed our eyes and folded our hands. I can't remember the actual words we prayed, but, as I stood up from my wooden chair, an idea popped into my head.

I went straight to my laptop in the next room and posted an announcement on our website. The Diospi Suyana "$100,000 Campaign" would run for the next three days and all proceeds would go towards making the hospital ready for its scheduled grand opening. I explained our current dire financial straits. Anyone wishing to contribute was asked to specify their donation as being for the "$100,000 Campaign."

The response was not long in coming. By Thursday evening, three days later, two-thirds of the money had already been received and another $20,000 was on its way from other supporters. Olaf Böttger wired the money from Germany to our account in Peru. In the following week, even more contributions rolled in, all earmarked for the "$100,000 Campaign." All told, the campaign netted $99,729 in emergency support for Diospi Suyana.

We invested every penny of the campaign in continued

I HAVE SEEN GOD

construction work. As successful as the campaign was, I wonder in retrospect whether I did the right thing. Maybe I should not have publicized our financial plight. Perhaps quiet, private prayer would have been even more effective and thus God's miracle all the greater.

As the last week started, we had the cash but were now running out of time. We would need to reserve Thursday and Friday for cleaning up, inside and out.

I will never forget that last Sunday before the dedication. On August 26, Tina and I walked through the empty rooms and corridors of the hospital. Half of the suspended ceilings were missing. The wind blew in through paneless windows, scattering dust down the hallways. We wondered what we could do to improve the visual impression the building would make on the big day. Was this the price of my optimism, arranging the date months ahead with the President's wife, without having a clue how far along we would actually be by the end of August? We had invested well over 3 million dollars in the construction of the hospital, and yet so much was still not finished. There was no way we could possibly set up our expensive equipment in this skeletal environment.

As had been the case so often in the last five years, we were just one step away from the edge – and failure. Our prayer to God for wisdom and help was more a cry of desperation. All day long, Tina and I planned in minute detail the coordination of the remaining work between the 100 construction workers and our thirty-four missionary volunteers. By evening, everyone had their marching orders.

In the next ninety-six hours, a dirty construction site was transformed inexplicably into a modern hospital. Everyone involved really outdid themselves in working together towards this seemingly impossible goal.

On Wednesday afternoon, I made several pressing phone calls to the senior Customs officials responsible for air freight. The German medical company Roche Inc. had just flown out lab equipment and reagents worth $200,000 so that we would be able to present them during the dedication ceremony. The truck would take at least twenty hours to reach Curahuasi, so it needed to depart from Lima as soon as possible. However, the Customs officials were not very reasonable and were holding the shipment because, as I was told, the documents I had submitted did not conform to their procedural requirements.

Enough was enough, and I exploded, "Either you release the Roche shipment immediately, or I will tell everyone at the dedication ceremony that you are blocking delivery! Did I mention that the President's wife will be there and that the ceremony is being televised?"

"You can't talk to us like that!" the Director of Customs retorted, and angrily hung up.

Five minutes later, the phone rang again.

"Dr. John, I just wanted to let you know that your shipment has now cleared Customs."

During the night, the last missing window panes arrived and were installed by the gray light of dawn. The Roche lab equipment made it as well. The courageous driver had driven for twenty-two hours almost non-stop. Bleary-eyed, our missionaries assembled a huge cake in the shape of the hospital. Barbara Klemenz had made twenty-three batches of cake mix for this amazing creation worthy of inclusion in *The Guinness Book of Records*, more than proving her expertise in cake-baking. Other volunteers set the tables or scrubbed at dirty marks on the walls and floors. The Peruvian television crews were already there and filmed our German nurses on their knees with cleaning rags. This act of humility and selfless service was to touch the nation two days later just as much as the colorful splendor of the ceremony itself.

45

Curtain Time for Diospi Suyana

Inevitably, there comes a time when there simply *is* no more time. We had reached zero hour.

After a mere three hours of sleep, I shot out of bed, awakened by the sound of torrential rain soaking Curahuasi. In my mind, I could see the sound board set up for the ceremony being swept away by currents of water. I ran over to the hospital with Olaf Böttger, who had come from Germany for this historic occasion. What a relief: one of the musicians had covered all the equipment and prevented a disaster!

Before we had even showered, Tina and I gave early-morning interviews on local radio stations and once again extended an invitation to all Curahuasinos to come and join in the festivities. We were so relieved to have come this far, and yet our heads were spinning with anticipation and unanswered questions. Would the President's wife really come all the way up from the capital? Would the Minister of Health be able to manage such a long journey with the two fractured ribs he had sustained in a car accident just the week before?

At 11 a.m. the amphitheater started to fill, and by midday 4,500 people were waiting in the hot sun for the celebrations to begin. The First Lady and the Minister arrived two hours behind schedule. At last we were ready to begin! We took a deep breath and stood, surrounded by an arc of nine television crews, to welcome our guests of honor.

The following four hours will remain with us forever. The First Lady and the Minister were visibly affected as they toured the hospital. They saw with their own eyes what the popular newspaper *La Republica* had hailed as the "Miracle of Curahuasi" – a modern medical facility in the mountains of southern Peru, equipped with the latest technology, including a CAT scanner and solar panels. In the future, up to 100,000 mountain Indios would seek treatment here each year.

The national anthems rang out. One speaker after another reflected profoundly on proverbial mountains being moved by faith. In my speech, I said that only God can make something out of nothing, and that all glory belonged to Him. The ceremony itself lasted three hours and the magic of this unique moment could be felt throughout the arena.

"All of Peru can learn from Diospi Suyana!" the First Lady said, as she told of our visit to her office the year before.

The photos and graphic simulation, once just data bits on a laptop computer, had exploded into life and become a reality. That same evening, many TV stations broadcast the news of Diospi Suyana throughout the nation. Millions of Peruvians heard a story that sounded as though it could only be a fairy tale. The ten-year dream that had taken my wife and me on a journey of 130,000 miles across Europe and the USA had finally come true. Diospi Suyana was indeed a monument to faith, our "Ebenezer," as it were, and only "hither by [His] help" had we come.

The next day 1,200 visitors walked in awe through the long halls of the hospital, surely unable to fathom or appreciate the purpose of the many machines they saw. But one thing they understood clearly as it echoed in their hearts: this hospital was for them.

46

From the Mountain Top Down to the Valley

J ournalists and reporters who had taken part in the dedication ceremony did their best to spread the news about Diospi Suyana, realizing it was extraordinary among the hospitals in South America. The pictures from the grand event went via several television networks to other South American countries, including Brazil.

What had seemed like foolishness and naïvety (i.e. the "trusting God" part) on the day of the ground-breaking in May 2005 had turned in just two years into an epic story of success. The mayor of a district of Lima sent us a letter of congratulation, in which she wrote that Peru was not the same after August 31, 2007. A student from Lima sent an email declaring, "I came to Curahuasi with great expectations, but what I saw exceeded them all!" And then there was Mr. Wawrik, a representative from the Braun-Melsungen Group who had attended the festivities. A few months later, he described those hours in Curahuasi as one of the most impressive experiences of his life.

I had invited many company managers and politicians to Curahuasi for the dedication of Diospi Suyana. Most of them sat on the stage as guests of honor and were able to follow the program from up close. The vivid proceedings touched not only their hearts, but also their wallets. No sooner had they returned home than many of them made significant decisions to support our work. Carlos Vargas of the Neptunia shipping company extended his assistance from the ten containers initially proffered to an unlimited number. IMPSAT doubled our bandwidth cap. And, without any hesitation, Guido del Castillo invested another $40,000 in digging the first ever well in the Abancay Province. It was dug on the hospital grounds, right behind the amphitheater, Señor Feliu von Josfel donated 800 new lamps worth $41,000, and told us that any additional ones we might need would be made available to us at cost. Evidently the grand opening of an incomplete hospital was the perfect impetus for getting the remaining work done.

For all those who were present, August 31 was an unforgettable "mountain-top" experience. Tina and I were expecting the prevailing exhilaration to carry over to our staff meeting the following Monday. We thought we would spend the time that evening praising God for His many blessings. How wrong we were...

We had barely begun the meeting when one staff member launched a bitter complaint about the amount of work she had been expected to do in the last few days, saying that the pace we had set had been inhuman. In the next breath, she lamented moving to Peru so early, as the previous months had been a waste of her time. She was oblivious to the contradiction in her two statements.

Another woman added that, in the hectic preparations of the last few days, she had not felt that we had taken adequate care of her. These comments set the tone for the rest of the meeting, and more began to verbalize their own frustration, annoyance, and resentment in what became a tidal wave of negativity. Since Tina and I bore ultimate responsibility for Diospi Suyana, all the pent-up discontent of our staff was dumped on us like a can of trash.

Tina, in particular, was completely taken aback. While I was on the road, she had always done her best to take care of each individual, promoting harmony and welcoming newcomers. Like me, she had given all she had, pushing herself to the limit for months on end. Despite the chronic fatigue and adversity, God had helped us keep the project going. We had not really expected our staff to thank us, but nor had we expected to be attacked. Did they really grasp the scope of Diospi Suyana? Could they empathize at all with the sacrifices Tina and I had made over the last five years?

We stood strong and maintained our composure, but that night after the meeting Tina sat on her bed and wept for two solid hours. I recalled the words of Heinrich Finger, head of the United German Mission Aid. What he said to me back in 2002 had puzzled me greatly at the time, but I understood it all too well now.

"Klaus, if you really build this hospital, you will be a lonely man in Curahuasi."

47

The Hospital Will (Never) Be Finished

The last of our visitors had packed up and left. The remains of the once-festive decorations fluttered in the breeze around the amphitheater. Under the leadership of Udo Klemenz, the workers picked up their tools once again, and it wasn't long before heavy construction equipment resumed its thunderous roar across the site. The dedication ceremony was fading into memory.

The library, the physical therapy room, and the pharmacy still lacked suspended ceilings. Brave men shinnied up ladders and got to work. A large container from Switzerland brought hundreds of pieces of furniture, which were painstakingly arranged throughout the hospital. In the chapel, the master craftsmen set to work on the twenty unfinished stained-glass windows. Many rooms had floor tiles yet to be installed. The painters certainly enjoyed a sense of "job security," as there was several months' worth of work remaining. The hospital kitchen was a major project in and of itself. During the dedication, we had used white boards to cover the doorway to the yawning black hole that bore no resemblance to the functional mess it was to become. The hospital exterior still required plenty of attention as well: we needed more wall braces on the cliff side, and initial construction of a guard shack for the front gate of the property.

Despite our doubts, the financial support from our friends all over the world did not decline. Nor did interest in Diospi Suyana: we were actually seeing an increase in the number of daily hits on our website!

On September 2, *El Comercio*, the leading newspaper in Peru, ran a comprehensive report on Diospi Suyana in the Sunday edition. The headline read: "The Hospital of Faith Has Opened Its Doors." Over a million readers rejoiced in the news, and calls began coming in with requests for details of our projected services.

The actual opening date was a hot topic of discussion among the Diospi Suyana staff. Many wanted the doors to open sooner rather than later, and were champing at the bit to begin working with patients. Others, perhaps more cautiously, favored an opening date later in the year.

In our last newsletter, I had boldly stated that the clinic was to be operational by October. It is absolutely critical to maintain credibility, particularly when soliciting support from others, so I was bound and determined that the doors of Diospi Suyana would open before the release of the next newsletter.

At ten minutes to 9 o'clock, on the morning of October 22, the moment had finally arrived. An elderly Quechua Indio pushed through the glass front door and stepped over the threshold to become our first patient. Nearly two and a half years after the ground-breaking ceremony, Diospi Suyana was officially open for business. As the patients streamed through the corridors, the workers continued with their various finishing projects.

"What do you think?" I asked Udo Klemenz. "When will we finally have finished building?"

"Klaus," he said knowingly, "don't kid yourself. A hospital like this will *never* be finished."

48

Antroferno, Luciana, and All the Others

Antroferno stared dully at the mud wall. The room had no windows, and the one small shaft of light that seemed to fight the gloom slipped in where a wooden door had been cracked open. He lay on a filthy mattress, emaciated and covered with painful sores. A paraplegic, Antroferno had given up all hope of recovery. He lay waiting, perhaps even hoping, for death. If this was "living," why should his life be valued?

One day, his cousin came to visit from Cusco. As her eyes gradually adjusted to the murky room, she took a deep breath.

"Antroferno, animals have a better life than you do," she whispered, appalled. "I will take you away from here – to the Diospi Suyana Hospital!"

The young man nodded his head slowly in consent, but said nothing. He had never heard of the hospital, but anywhere had to be better than the hellhole in which he was living.

Outpatient care was up and running more smoothly by the day, so we decided to open our inpatient care and operating facilities in May 2008. Antroferno was one of the first patients to be admitted to the hospital. The nurses placed him in a clean bed, washed him carefully, and cleaned his wounds. He looked considerably better, his sores covered by the sterile white bandages. Even the stench from the festering had dissipated. When had he ever experienced such love and care? Antroferno could not believe his good fortune.

He looked around the room in wonder: at 175 square feet, there was space enough for four patients. The white walls and tile floors were immaculate. Yellow curtains hung at the windows. There were ports in the wall for oxygen and extraction. He had never seen anything like it. Fresh air flowed into the room through ventilation points in the ceiling. Next to the door, which was wide enough to accommodate a hospital bed, there was a large closet with multiple doors. A whole section was just for him; at least, that is what the nurse had said. Right next door was a place where patients could enjoy a warm shower each morning. People told him that energy from the sun was used to heat the water. Antroferno thought the hospital was nothing short of heaven.

In the coming days, doctors clothed in white gathered around his bed, speaking Spanish with a foreign accent and regarding their new patient with compassion. Nobody made any disparaging remarks, yelled at him, or treated him with anything other than kindness and respect. They discussed the best possible treatment for him, including nutrition, wound care, and surgery. There was never any mention of money. Antroferno had neither soles nor dollars. If no relative was found who could assist with paying the medical costs, the hospital would assume financial responsibility for all services rendered.

Antroferno remained in the care of nurses for six long months. It took two major operations to close up the ulcers on his buttocks. When he was finally discharged shortly before

Christmas, his wounds were completely healed. Despite the paraplegia, Antroferno returned home a new man. He had even learned to read and write during his stay at Diospi Suyana!

We were able to help many patients in the first few months after the hospital had opened. Often, our patients' lives were permanently changed. Rolando was one such example. He had spent his childhood growing up in the slums of Lima. This handsome young man seemed bright, and at twenty could well have worked his way up the ladder of success, but for one serious handicap. Owing to a scalding accident as a child, Rolando had completely lost mobility in his left shoulder. The scar tissue resulting from the burns caused his arm to be frozen stiffly at shoulder level, leaving him with essentially zero range of motion. A missionary alerted us to Rolando's need and paid for him to take the bus from Lima to Curahuasi.

Visiting surgeon Matthias Stephani wasted no time. He mobilized the joint and conducted a skin graft procedure. The post-op physical therapy was in the very capable hands of Simone Klingelhöfer. A photo of Rolando leaving the hospital shows him stretching his left arm up to the sky – a sign of miraculous victory!

The altitude in the Andes causes a great deal of fluctuation in temperature. Even on warm days, as soon as the sun sets beyond the mountains, it becomes quite cold. Unlike Europe and the US, none of the houses have heating, and many families cannot afford window panes. As a result, many of the Quechua suffer from respiratory illnesses, especially during the winter months of June, July, and August. A common cold passes quickly enough, but bronchitis or pneumonia can result in a chronic lack of oxygen and an often slow, agonizing death. When Luciana was admitted to the hospital with breathing difficulties, tests indicated dangerously low levels of oxygen saturation in her blood. She was hooked up to a ventilator immediately and transferred to the ICU, where nurses Stefan Hofer and Michael Mörl spent anxious hours at her bedside. After two days on the ventilator, she was out of danger. Our well-equipped ICU, along with skilled and caring staff, literally saved her life.

Compassionate, high-quality nursing care and effective medical treatment led Diospi Suyana to earn a very good reputation. Word of mouth spread quickly, as grateful patients shared their experiences with family and friends. As a result, the number of people seeking care has skyrocketed. There are often days when there are more waiting in line than can possibly be seen by our current cadre of doctors. More are always needed, and it has become my priority to find those called to serve at Diospi Suyana.

49

President Sherlock Holmes

Without question, our doctors and nurses were doing excellent work. And yet we were all operating in a gray area on the fringes of legality, for neither the hospital as an institution nor the foreign volunteers providing services had any kind of license to practice medicine in the country of Peru. Tina and I did our best to collect any and all documentation that might be required for Peruvian licensure, as we recognized our nebulous status as a clear Achilles heel. A single mistake in the operating room or perceived incident of malpractice could unleash a tidal wave of calamity from which we had no protection.

Diospi Suyana had enemies. Most often, these were people out for their own personal or political gain, and their allegations had no basis in reality. For example, one contingent had spread vicious rumors that the mission hospital was involved with child trafficking and the sale of human organs. A politician who had narrowly lost in the 2006 Apurímac presidential race was particularly malicious in his accusations. Of course, he didn't really believe the lies he was spreading, but he had hoped to engage the trust and political backing of the mountain farmers by feeding their natural wariness of the unknown. This same man owned a large liquor factory and made a great deal of money from the sale of alcohol. We at the hospital saw much suffering related to alcoholism, and we worked hard to counter the effects of such substance abuse. But fewer drunks on the streets quickly translated to a loss of profit for the factory. In retaliation, a smear campaign was launched, again attempting to undermine the faith that people were putting in the Diospi Suyana Hospital.

A number of doctors in Abancay and Cusco saw some of their wealthy clientele migrate to Diospi Suyana. A high-quality international hospital certainly doesn't just attract the poor. Peruvian friends warned us that these doctors were eagerly waiting for some trouble to befall us, reducing the unwelcome competition in their field.

Our dealings with the national health authority, DIRESA, were extremely tough and were yielding very little progress. Two doctors from Abancay were currently engaged in a legal battle for the position of director, so it was no wonder we were getting nowhere, despite having submitted an application for a hospital operating license – hundreds of pages long – back in November 2007. Four months went by and we had yet to receive an answer. In the course of a visit to the Ministry of Health in Lima, I learned that the new Health Minister would be touring the province of Abancay in the near future. I had never actually met Garrido Lecca in person, but I had heard a lot about him. He was the quintessential rising star on the political scene. As a sharp electoral campaign strategist, he had won the confidence of the President. The early years of his brilliant career had taken him to both Harvard and MIT. He was undoubtedly highly intelligent, and had good business sense too, as indicated by his successful management of a Peruvian fast-food chain. He, however, took the most personal pride in his accomplishments as a children's book author and film director.

I needed to get this man on the Diospi Suyana team. I composed a long email, officially inviting him to our hospital. During telephone conversations with his office staff, I pointedly mentioned our good relationship with the First Lady of Peru. To attract even more attention, I sent copies of my email exchanges with the Peruvian media. My efforts seemed to bear fruit. I was given a copy of Mr. Lecca's travel itinerary, and was thrilled to see that he had included a visit to Diospi Suyana as the last item on the last day.

The Minister of Health was due at our hospital at 8 p.m. on March 5. Our job was to showcase our work in the best possible light. I put everyone on high alert, and we scurried about tidying up in anticipation of his imminent arrival. Our missionary ladies prepared a mouth-watering buffet of soup, sandwiches, and cake. We gathered in the hospital chapel at 7 p.m. to pray. If God would give His blessing to our plans, I would mark this special day on my calendar with three crosses.

The ministerial convoy consisted of six vehicles packed with thirty government officials from Lima. Engineer Sifuente was one of them. He had attended the hospital's dedication ceremony, and now kept me up to date on the convoy's progress as they traveled towards Curahuasi. As usual, the last items on the itinerary were behind schedule. The Minister would not reach the hospital at 8 p.m., as originally planned, but would most likely be delayed until about 9 p.m. This was actually quite welcome news, as three workers were still in the process of hanging up yellow and red signs indicating the various departments throughout the hospital corridors.

At 11 p.m., the Minister and his entourage finally arrived at the main entrance. Fifty members of Diospi Suyana welcomed them warmly in the waiting area. Garrido Lecca was wearing a poncho and had evidently been fast asleep through the journey over the mountain pass. Mr. Sifuente told me they would only be able to stay and see the hospital for about ten minutes as they were so far behind schedule.

If ever there was an unfavorable combination of factors, this was it: an exhausted Minister under extreme pressure of time in the middle of the night. But, for God, these details are irrelevant. He alone orchestrates every circumstance as He sees fit. Things can always change in the blink of an eye, and if we trust Him, we can expect Him to act – no matter what.

The Minister had just spied the long buffet table.

"Muchachos!" he called out as he turned to his delegates, "there is food here!"

There was a murmur of gratitude as the officials approached the spread. As I learned later, the group had had nothing to eat all day.

They filled up their plates and took a seat in the auditorium. I welcomed them cordially on behalf of Diospi Suyana, personally acknowledging the Minister and calling attention to the two things I knew we had in common: not only were we the same age, but we had also both studied at Harvard. My words – plus a strong cup of coffee – appeared to give the Minister a second wind. I knew he had had a very long day and that concentrating would be a challenge, but I prayed he could attend to the forty-five-minute presentation I was about to share. He did indeed, and by the end Garrido Lecca understood well what our hospital was all about.

As I passed the microphone to him shortly before midnight, he made references to faith in God, and even quoted from Psalm 23.

"How can I help you?" he asked.

This is the question I had hoped all along that he would ask.

"We desperately need an operating license for our hospital!"

With sudden inspiration, I continued, "We would also be very grateful if you could help us get an audience with the President."

Our eyes met and Garrido Lecca nodded.

"Yes, I will use my influence on your behalf."

Tina and I then led the Minister and his entourage on a tour of the entire hospital. As they followed us through the corridors, Mr. Lecca kept repeating a single word: "Spectacular!"

At 1 a.m., we finally shook hands in farewell. Michael Mörl presented the Minister with one of his homemade loaves of bread, fresh and delicious, to remind him of our German roots, which had found such unexpected new soil in this remote region, and in such an amazing way. As the convoy vehicles pulled away, we returned to the chapel. We had previously prayed for God's help; now we wanted to thank Him for His provision.

The Minister kept his word. Two weeks later, Diospi Suyana was in possession of a permanent operating license. This had been a major challenge, but we still weren't in the clear. We each needed our individual licensure to practice medicine in Peru.

On the recommendation of the Deputy Health Minister, I had spoken to the Dean of the Medical School at Federico Villareal University about our dilemma. Dr. Cordero was quite positive.

"Dr. John, I think we will soon be able to provide you with the reciprocal licensure you need."

He sounded so sincere, like a man who could make things happen.

"Hand in your documentation," he continued. "I'll take care of it. This is all just a formality."

Happy to have finally found a solution, I believed every word the Dean said. For an entire year, I handed him one document after another, as he requested.

In March 2008, the Dean swore to me, "Dr. John, you will have your certificate in two weeks!"

But, in South America, giving your word is considered far less binding than it is in other parts of the world. The Dean didn't, or perhaps couldn't, follow through. There was a festering hostility towards foreigners in the committee responsible for reviewing our applications. Despite the fact that Tina was a scholarship holder of the German National Academic Foundation, which selects the top 1 percent of all German students, and despite my own studies at Yale and Harvard, our formidable qualifications were completely ignored. The panel did not even seem to be impressed by the fact that we had built one of the most modern hospitals in the entire country, at a cost of about 10 million dollars. On April 22, we were officially informed that the University had declined to grant us the reciprocal license for medical practice in Peru. What a disappointment! We were still standing there empty-handed.

On the night of Garrido Lecca's visit to Diospi Suyana, I had blurted out a bold request for an audience with the President. I followed up on this unremittingly during my regular visits to Lima. Maybe the President himself could help us? On April 23, we received notice that the President had agreed to meet Tina and me on Saturday, April 26. Dr. David Brady had been accompanying me during the previous week in Lima, and we were miraculously able to get his name added to the very short guest list. The appointment itself was a complete surprise, since the European–South American Summit was scheduled to take place two weeks later. National leaders from all over the world, including Germany, would be meeting in the Peruvian capital. All of Lima had only one subject on their minds: the Summit.

Tina had intended to fly to Lima on the Friday afternoon before our meeting, but her last-minute plans fell through. She got stuck in Cusco and her only option was to fly out early Saturday. Morning flights between Cusco and Lima are often cancelled or delayed owing to inclement weather, so we were biting our nails until the last minute, hoping her plane would depart on time.

I suppose it was almost a quiet premonition that had inspired me to buy a new brown suit just ten days earlier. David and I stood outside the Presidential Palace, dressed to the nines, and looking at our watches every two minutes. It was a quarter to ten, and still there was no sign of Tina. We were unable to reach her by cell phone either. We kept hoping she had made it to Lima safely. Dr. Chorrea from the Ministry of Health joined us. He too had flexed his personal ties to the President to make this meeting happen. We could tell this was no ordinary morning.

But where was Tina? Restless, I paced up and down the street. At the last possible second, my cell phone rang. It was Tina. After a wild cab ride, she had arrived at the Palace and was somewhere around the other side of the building, trying to catch her breath. I was inordinately relieved. Her charisma would surely warm the President's heart.

We knocked at the heavy door and were led into the official reception hall. It had no windows, but the golden wall lights filled the room with their radiant glow. Two photographers had taken up position near the wall, ready to capture this great honor for us, and thus for Diospi Suyana. A master of ceremonies directed us to our assigned seats on the sofas and explained how the meeting would progress.

At 10 a.m. on the dot, a large side door opened and President Alan García entered with his wife, Pilar Nores de García. They welcomed us graciously, and then joined us on the red upholstered couches. My presentation could begin.

Prior to this day, we "knew" Alan García only from what we heard on TV. He was a gifted speaker, and even his political adversaries had to acknowledge his extraordinary eloquence. But now he was silent, listening attentively.

"Dr. John, you are closer to God than I am," the President remarked as the presentation ended. "Is there anything I can do to help you with your work? Do you need anything at all?"

"Well, we have been trying for over a year to get reciprocal licensure to practice medicine here in Peru."

My "hint" was enough.

"I would be glad to intervene on your behalf!"

The President's response was exactly what I had hoped for. As our time came to an end, the photographers snapped a few group shots to capture the occasion, and we said our goodbyes in a friendly, relaxed manner.

As we descended the steps to the foyer, we were suddenly surrounded by a host of journalists. Some represented the national TV station and others, various newspapers. Directing their spotlights and microphones at us, they inquired about the outcome of the meeting that had just taken place. As the cameras rolled, I described our humanitarian efforts as a true work of faith, and thanked the President and his wife for the unique honor they had just bestowed on us.

In the afternoon, we flew to Cusco and then drove home to Curahuasi. Exhausted from the stress of the day, yet exhilarated by the actual events, we changed out of our best clothes. We had just experienced the greatest honor of our lives.

Alan García did not forget his promise. He instructed his lawyers to do whatever was needed to ensure we would be licensed to practice medicine in Peru. The Minister of Health also intervened on our behalf. As a result of all these efforts, San Martin de Porres University finally recognized our German qualifications as meeting Peruvian standards three months later. In the second week of November, Tina and I took our places in the auditorium of the Peruvian Medical Association, and we were awarded our long-awaited reciprocal medical licenses, formally bestowed by the Dean of the *Colégio Médico del Perú*. We had fought hard for these documents for over a year and a half, and now we held them in our hands.

My thoughts drifted back to the previous April. Only four days after the shocking rejection by Federico Villareal University, the President of Peru himself had extended his full support. It is not the bureaucrats and technocrats who have the last word – it is God. Sometimes He answers our prayers quietly, almost imperceptibly. But when He wants to, He can initiate an audience in the Presidential Palace, complete with media coverage. What He wants done, will be done. There are no limits to His divine power. It is our responsibility to persist in prayer, to trust Him, and to thank Him from the bottom of our hearts.

50

Power On

The thunder boomed round the wide, high valley of Curahuasi, its apocalyptic echo amplified by the mountain slopes rising on both sides. The lightning flashed unremittingly, casting an eerie, ephemeral glow, while the wind whipped the flooding rain across the land. The storm's fury seemed to be concentrated right over Curahuasi. As the town's inhabitants cowered in their beds, they could clearly appreciate how little man could do against the elemental forces of nature. Generally, when we had a bad storm like this one, the town would go dark before too long. It was never obvious which generator had been the victim of a lightning strike, and usually it would take hours for a team from the electric company Electro Sur to restore power to the area. With few, if any, other options, the Curahuasinos simply pulled the covers up over their heads and waited till morning. Anybody really needing a light would just have to use a candle.

The lights went out at the hospital as well. Within seconds, strategically placed, battery-operated, emergency spotlights came on. They were supposed to last two hours, but we were dismayed to find they conked out after about twenty minutes. The night nurses stumbled their way through the pitch-black corridors, unable to see a thing, and tried to calm the patients. We were very fortunate that no one was in the ICU or in surgery on this stormy night. It is absolutely critical for a clinic to have an emergency generator that will kick in automatically and keep vital equipment running all night long. Patients' lives could depend on our being able to acquire this essential resource.

Back in March 2007, I had asked for a generator at the Peru Rotary Club's Annual Convention. I ended my presentation at the Sheraton Hotel in Lima by asking the crowd, "Would you like to help us?" The entire audience responded by rising to their feet in a standing ovation. I had pinned my hopes on Dr. Cantela, who headed up a large medical lab there in the capital, and who was also the chair of this prodigious convention involving forty Rotary Clubs from all over the country. His influence among the Rotarians would surely encourage the donation of a generator.

Dr. Cantela was familiar with the Diospi Suyana story and gladly offered his assistance. In his opinion, the German and Peruvian Rotarians should work together to provide the generator. In the event of such cooperation, Rotary International would match the amount raised by the two groups. The generator we needed would cost about $60,000 – a lot of money, but within reach if we all worked together.

Concurrently, I contacted several companies who were mining for copper, gold, and silver in the Apurímac region. The vast stores of precious metals and minerals beneath the earth's surface made the area a virtual "El Dorado." About eighty Peruvian and international companies have made a fortune from their exploits here. As part of their public relations efforts, all these companies have a department dedicated to social responsibility, although the brochures detailing related activities frequently cost more than has ever been invested by the companies in local schools or health clinics.

I HAVE SEEN GOD

The Extracta Group is an international consortium consisting of some of these companies. On September 20, 2007 – a Friday afternoon – I met the man responsible for PR at the Extracta Group. As I shared photos at a restaurant in Lima, Mr. Carceres was overwhelmingly convinced of the amazing effects of sacrificial giving.

"I really think we will be able to help get a generator for you!" he encouraged as he left.

A week later, it was clear that his supervisors had a different view: the management had no intention whatsoever of donating that kind of money to a humanitarian project.

One Sunday morning in October, eight of the managers from Intrepid Mines appeared on the hospital doorstep. I sensed a change in the air. Laurence Curtis, representing the Canadian contingent, led the group. They had heard about Diospi Suyana through business associates and were here to request a private tour of our facility. For two hours I showed them one department after another, casually mentioning every now and then how we needed a generator to keep all this expensive equipment running during the frequent power outages that plagued us during the rainy season.

"Here's my business card," Laurence Curtis said graciously. "Call me – I am sure that we can help you."

And call I did, taking him up on his generous offer. I phoned him repeatedly at his Toronto office, and sent one email after another, hoping against hope that he would follow through on his promise. Even the most well-meaning of intentions sometimes can be forgotten when it is time to put your money where your mouth is.

When the hospital opened its doors in October 2007, I had to really step up my efforts to obtain a generator. On November 8, Dr. Cantela invited me to meet his Rotary Club.

I knew $60,000 was a lofty goal, but I was optimistic about the details the Peruvian and German Rotarians would come up with in their joint venture to finance our request. As the Lima club shared the plan with me, I was crushed by the realization that they themselves intended to contribute only about $1,000 to the cause. Unfortunately, I have learned over time that the Peruvian elite often do not like using their own money to support charitable purposes, preferring instead to send out solicitation letters to friends and acquaintances all over the world.

I had knocked on every door. I had made hundreds of phone calls to multiple countries, and sent at least as many emails. But still I had made no progress whatsoever.

When David Brady and I presented our petition before the directors of the German–Peruvian Chamber of Commerce on April 22, 2008, we were sure that, this time, the outcome would finally be positive. The hospital was operational now, after all; it wasn't just a pipe dream. We had already treated thousands of patients. After seventeen television reports and forty articles in the press, Diospi Suyana was almost a household name throughout Peru. With Pilar Nores de García as one of our sponsors, we clearly had the approval of the President and his wife, so...

As I finished my presentation, the gentlemen around the table applauded. Together, they represented a considerable proportion of the Peruvian Gross National Product, and there was no doubt they could and would pay for a generator for us, even if only for publicity reasons.

But the President of the Chamber of Commerce, Dr. Schmidt, and the Managing Director, Jörg Zehnle, both put on their best poker face, imparting no decision or even inclination either way as we took our leave.

Four days later, we were once again in the Presidential Palace. Mr. García sent notice that he would meet with us shortly. As we waited, I called Mr. Zehnle to let him know where we were, in an attempt to pique his interest.

"If the Chamber of Commerce would donate the generator, the President himself could cut the red ribbon – with you standing right next to him!"

That appeared to do the trick – at least for the moment, Dr. Schmidt got on the phone himself to inquire where they might find a generator at an affordable price. Unfortunately, they could not find an option at less than $60,000, so in the end they turned me down.

Another week passed. I was out and about in Lima, visiting various government offices. At about 10 o'clock in the morning, as I was sitting in a cab, I noticed a scrap of white paper in my wallet. I must have been carrying it around with me for at least six months. On it was scribbled contact information for a Peruvian company called Detroit Diesel MTU, which makes components for generators and generally markets its products to mining companies. I had been seeking *funding* for a generator, and thus far had not contacted any business that might consider just giving us the generator itself. Undecided, I turned the paper over and over between my fingers. Should I call, on the off chance? What did I have to lose? As the cab driver sped round the residential blocks as though on a Formula One racetrack, I gave Detroit Diesel a call and was given an appointment for 5 p.m.

Whenever I am in Lima, my schedule is crammed full, with every appointment beginning right on the heels of the one before. This visit was no different. At 5 p.m., I was just leaving the Ministry of Health. There was no way I could make it to Detroit Diesel in a reasonable amount of time, so I called to cancel. It probably didn't matter: I had not been expecting much to come from that meeting anyway.

"I am sorry, I can't make it today. It would be 6 p.m. before I got there."

"That doesn't matter at all," replied a friendly voice. "If need be, I'll wait *two* hours for you. Please come by."

You didn't need to be a rocket scientist to figure out why the engineer was being so kind and obliging. Clearly, he assumed I was a potential customer with money to spend. Who would want to miss out on such a sale? In neither of my two calls had I mentioned that, as a mission hospital, we didn't actually want to *purchase* anything at all.

With its 8 million inhabitants and corresponding traffic, the streets of Lima were nearly always a challenge to negotiate. During the 5 o'clock rush hour, they were an absolute nightmare. At its worst, it could take as much as two hours to get from the north to the south of the city.

The cab driver was highly skilled and maneuvered easily through the stop-and-go traffic, weaving in and out of lanes and inventing entirely new ones to get past the endless lines of cars. As I sat in the back, my thoughts started to slide down a dark path, spiraling into negativity and approaching despair. I had tried everything for an entire year, just attempting to get a generator donated. I had always come up with nothing. Everything thus far had been a complete waste of time and energy.

Dusk was falling as the taxi pulled up in front of 2020 Avenida Argentina. I paid the driver and stepped slowly onto the sidewalk. I knew it was completely ridiculous to walk into a Peruvian company, holding out my hands and saying "Pretty please." At best, they would simply laugh me off.

I set down my laptop case and took a deep breath. I normally had at least two contingency plans mentally sketched out, but this time I had come to the end of my rope. I had no other ideas and nowhere else to go. I felt an inner "nudge" and gave in to the sudden urge to pray. With lines of cars behind me and the Detroit Diesel property fence in front of me, I cried aloud in desperation:

"God, You know I've tried everything this past year! I don't know what else to do! Please, give me a miracle!"

There are all kinds of prayers: prescribed prayers, unctuous prayers, spiritless prayers, prayers of duty, and prayers of habit. Mine was none of these. Mine came from the depths of the soul of a man in a hopeless situation. I finally grasped that only God could provide the answer.

As I looked at the entrance, I noticed the security guard for the first time. He must have heard me crying out in German, and undoubtedly thought I was crazy. On the one hand, such a public display was a bit embarrassing. On the other, I knew that I had done the right thing – in fact, the *only* thing I could do under the circumstances.

Mr. Mayorga really had stayed late in his office to wait for me, just as he had said he would. He followed my entire forty-five-minute presentation without the slightest hint of boredom or impatience. No sooner had I finished than I blurted out an awkward apology.

"I am sure you were expecting a customer, not a beggar. I am so sorry!"

"No, no, not at all. I am glad I heard your story. God means a lot to me too, and I would like to help you. The question is – how?"

We had connected, and were now remarkably on the same wavelength. I had heard that the owner of the company was a rather caustic, unapproachable octogenarian, so Mr. Mayorga suggested:

"Maybe we should approach his son. He might be more receptive to your request."

He gave me a ride back to Miraflores and we arranged to stay in touch. At the end of this very long day, May 23, hope had finally begun to dawn.

Six days later, I was back at Detroit Diesel once more. Luis Pineda, Sales Director, was to be my point of contact. He was younger than I, and very obviously in a great hurry. Nevertheless, I raced through my presentation with him, speaking so fast that I was swallowing whole words.

"What you have built in Apurímac is fantastic!" he exclaimed. "The boss must see this!"

Then he excused himself and scurried away.

On June 6, 2008, at 3 a.m., a driver took me the eighty miles to Cusco for the first flight out to Lima. I was scheduled to be in the office of the owner of Detroit Diesel at 10 a.m. sharp. Far away in Curahuasi, several missionaries were fervently praying for God's blessing on this pivotal meeting.

The old man beckoned me in and allowed me to set up my laptop right on his desk. He even came around to my side and took a seat next to me, nodding to indicate he was ready for me to begin my presentation.

"You know, Mr. Salhuana," I began thoughtfully, "all my life I have wondered whether there was a God. This story answers that question."

I intentionally spoke more slowly than usual. The presentation stretched to a full hour, and yet, despite Mr. Salhuana's advanced years, he paid full attention. Whenever I share the story of Diospi Suyana, I aim to touch the hearts of the audience. This time, I appeared to have succeeded.

Carl Saulhana cleared his throat audibly and came straight to the point.

"Dr. John, my son owns a quarter of this company. For this reason, I must speak with him first, but you will have our decision within the week."

When my cell phone rang four days later, I was back in Curahuasi, somewhere in the hospital, and it took me a few moments to realize who was calling.

"Dr. John, Salhuana here. I just wanted to let you know that we will donate the emergency generator. After hearing you speak about your hospital, I had no choice."

The conversation ended as abruptly as it had begun. I sank into a chair and remembered my prayer at the gates of Detroit Diesel. In the darkest of hours, my desperate supplication to God had been heard.

Over the next few months, a colossal generator weighing nearly four tons was manufactured especially for Diospi Suyana. It was designed to start up within thirty seconds of a power outage. Its capacity was sufficient to sustain all the electronic equipment in the hospital. Detroit Diesel MTU had never made such a large donation as this generator, worth at least $60,000. But then it's likely that nobody had ever cried out to God for help at their company gates before, either.

51

Waste Not, Want Not

When spectacular things happen in answer to prayer, we have little difficulty ascribing the miracle to God – assuming we believe in Him to begin with. But sometimes we forget that His hand takes care of the little things too. The Bible describes God as a loving Father who is interested in the most "trivial" and "mundane" concerns; all we need to do is lay them at His feet. Our current dilemma involved the efficient, sanitary disposal of human waste. Dare we even bring up such a basic matter in prayer?

If you have ever been in hospital, you will know that a bedpan is a very useful tool for the bedridden when they need to answer nature's call. But have you ever wondered how the contents of that pan are disposed of? For the last eighty years or so, hospitals have had the benefit of specially designed bedpan washing machines. In clinic vernacular, these are known as "bedpan flushers."

This was the exact piece of equipment I now sought to procure for our hospital. I needed three of them, in fact. On November 19, I arrived at the corporate office of Kodra in Stuttgart, laptop case in hand. Kodra has been a principal force behind the development and distribution of this practical device. As always, I had committed this visit to God in prayer.

Chief Executive Gerhard Bretschneider was rather busy

that day, but he found time to attend my Diospi Suyana presentation. After all, I was a potential customer, and there was money to be made. Or so he thought. Towards the end of the story, Mr Bretschneider was beginning to realize that I was not the lucrative prospect he had anticipated. I had obviously not traveled all the way from Peru to actually *pay* for three bedpan flushers. He was visibly annoyed.

"Dr. John, I thought you had come to Kodra as a paying customer. You don't get anything for nothing here!"

Embarrassed, I remained silent. I felt like someone who had snuck in under false pretenses. I am generally quick-witted and silver-tongued, but on this occasion I was at a complete loss for words.

"I'll show you one of the machines so you will at least know what we are talking about," Mr. Bretschneider growled.

He led me to the second floor and pointed towards a rather large plexiglass contraption. I grasped that this was a demonstration model displayed at medical trade fairs. The clear construction allowed curious observers to see just how the interior water jets forcibly flushed even the biggest of brown blobs away into the sewage system. The flushing fountains in the demo structure were rather entertaining, but I had not failed to notice how simple the construction actually was. It was basically just a box with a rack on which to put the bedpan, and a few water nozzles.

"Mr. Bretschneider, this looks like the kind of machine that would last forever. We would be so grateful if you would even consider donating used bedpan flushers."

That proposal certainly missed its mark. Mr. Bretschneider gestured dismissively.

"We don't have used equipment here. Any machines that are returned are repaired immediately, cleaned, and resold."

He was adamant that there was no solution here in Stuttgart for our waste-disposal problem.

"Could you perhaps call the warehouse? Maybe there is used equipment still in there somewhere."

Mr. Bretschneider was piqued by my unyielding persistence.

"No, I do *not* need to call the warehouse. I *know* we don't have anything in there!"

I had to admit that this agitated executive before me would logically know quite a bit more about the contents of his warehouse than I did, but still I kept on.

"Mr. Bretschneider, I am asking you as a favor: please call the warehouse."

Scowling, he reached for his cell phone and punched a number. There was a short exchange with a colleague in another part of the building. As Mr. Bretschneider hung up, his eyes grew wide, an odd expression of both amazement and confusion appearing on his face.

"My colleague has just informed me that there are three used bedpan washing machines in a corner of the warehouse. This is incredible!"

Mr. Bretschneider shook his head in disbelief, genuinely shocked by this revelation.

"Mr. Bretschneider, do you know – I see this happen time and time again," I said softly, "because I pray for God's blessing before every meeting, every appointment. I know the outcome is always in His hands."

He looked at me thoughtfully, but said nothing.

Of course, we both wanted to take a closer look at these three bedpan flushers that had somehow miraculously materialized in the warehouse without the boss's knowledge. We strode through the warehouse, heading straight for the back left corner. There they were, plain as day.

The colleague with whom Mr. Bretschneider had spoken on the phone was there waiting for us.

"I had hoped to sell Dr. John three bedpan flushers today," Mr. Bretschneider called out to his colleague as we approached, "but we're going to let him have these three here for nothing." This drastic shift in attitude and effect was enough to make one wonder if there weren't possibly *two* Mr. Bretschneiders running around. Surely this couldn't be the same man who had shot down my initial request so vehemently?

"We will clean them, make sure they are working properly, and then send them off to you, with some spare parts." The magnanimity of Baden-Württemberg was shining through. "Where do you want them delivered?"

"Bedpan flusher" (*Steckbeckenspülgerät* in German) is almost a tongue-twister for me, and certainly not a word I use every day. But our hospital now has four of them. Kodra remains faithful in its service, and I have no doubt that these machines will be in perfect working order even twenty years from now.

The value of this gift far exceeds the monetary cost. It showed me – and I hope you as well – that we can pray about *any* of our concerns. God is faithful – even with feces...

52

Salzburg, São Paulo, Washington

In the spring of 2004, a ramp had proved very useful as Detlev Hofmann and I rolled the four old anesthesia machines straight up and into the van. We patted each other on the back, and that was it – the first pieces of donated equipment were on their way. The antiquated pieces of apparatus were certainly not the "latest and greatest," but they would do the job in Curahuasi just as well as they had for the past fifteen years at the municipal clinic in Wiesbaden.

Our anesthesiologist, Tove Hohaus, had not been shy about voicing her opinion in February 2007, when she first laid eyes on the equipment stored in Darmstadt.

"If I am supposed to work with these, I am going to need a user manual," she asserted, frowning.

I didn't like her tone. I was in the middle of packing other cases for the container and wasn't up for dealing with unproductive negativity. On the other hand, as a surgeon, I had to admit that these machines were more archaic than I would want in my own operating room.

A plan started to form at the back of my mind, although it certainly would not be easy to get off the ground. I wanted to do everything possible to get the directors of Dräger International on board in support of Diospi Suyana. The Dräger Corporation had been a huge name in anesthetic equipment for generations. I learned that Stefan Dräger now ran the company, which boasted a workforce of 10,000 and annual sales figures upwards of $2 billion.

I asked Dr. Pfahlert, a former manager of Roche, Inc., for his assistance in making the initial contact. Before transferring from Roche to Dräger in June 2007, he had arranged for three sets of laboratory equipment to be donated to Diospi Suyana. He had only a brief stint at Dräger, but it was long enough for him to become familiar with the inner workings of the company. He told me that Stefan Dräger's wife was extremely involved with social action and humanitarian causes. Although the titbits of information he shared were helpful, he was unable to get me through the doors of the corporate headquarters in Lübeck. Efforts by the head of a medical–technical company in the Rhine-Main area also failed.

Weeks passed, and I ultimately ended up calling Dräger myself. I had hoped to be put straight through to the CEO himself, but I was unable to get further than the lady at the reception desk. She explained that Mr. Dräger was away, but then caught me completely off-guard by giving me his direct email address. An hour later, a message was on its way to Mr. Dräger, who was on the Baltic coast at the time. I didn't really anticipate a personal response from him, but I have learned over time that once a matter is given over to God in prayer, literally anything can happen.

In early 2008, I did in fact receive an invitation to Lübeck, where Michael Karsta, the manager of the South America, Africa, and Asia divisions, would meet me.

March 12 was a cold, dismal, rainy day, but fortunately I did not have far to drive from Hamburg. I hurried to the main building, anxious to get out of the winter chill that seemed to penetrate to my bones. As I thawed out with a cup of hot coffee,

Michael Karsta and his colleague, Koen Paredis, explained the day's schedule. I was welcome to share my presentation with them in the afternoon, but Dräger had something they wanted to show me first.

I was escorted into a special room and asked to lie down under a huge block of stone approximately thirty inches thick. A steel rope suspended the 950-pound mass just a foot over my head. A deep, masculine voice came through the loudspeaker, pontificating on the need for trust. Apparently I must have had "trust" in the strength of the rope, for I stayed still, even though I would not have survived if the block of stone had fallen.

After about forty-five seconds of this, the illustration was over and I was still in one piece.

"By the way," I remarked to the Dräger representatives as I jumped up from the hard floor, "trust is my motto too. Our Diospi Suyana Hospital in Peru was founded on trust in God."

This unusual display was designed to orient potential customers to the Dräger history of excellence, which spanned five generations. The purpose, I realized immediately, was to instill a strong trust in Dräger's products. Mr. Karsta and Mr. Paredis devoted a lot of time to me that day, even though I was not a real customer. I assumed they already knew why I had come, based on my note to Stefan Dräger.

Just before lunch, a young woman came by. She seemed quite interested in learning more about Diospi Suyana and asked a number of questions. Sometimes I just don't put two and two together, and I didn't think much about who the woman might have been. We chatted amicably, and I invited her to my presentation at 2 p.m. She regretfully had to decline, and wished me a good remainder of the day at Dräger. It wasn't until later in the afternoon that I finally realized that this mystery woman was Claudia Dräger, Stefan's wife.

In the afternoon, I was given the opportunity to share my presentation with Michael Karsta and Koen Paredis. As they stared, riveted to the screen, I could see that the photos of Diospi Suyana had really got to them. On the way to the corporate office, I had planned to ask for just one new anesthesia machine. Far away in Peru, Tove Hohaus was praying for two. When I witnessed how affected these men had been by the Diospi Suyana story, I threw caution to the wind and asked for four. My wife had encouraged me to ask for a respirator for children and a resuscitation table for newborns as well. The way I saw it, I could get a "yes" only if I actually asked the questions. If I held my tongue, the answer would be "no" by default. So ask I did!

"We will ask Mrs. Dräger to donate all these items."

Mr. Karsta's response was concise but promising.

As the week went by, my hopes began to swell with each passing day. Surely the Dräger family would honor our request. On March 19, Michael Karsta sent me the glorious news that Claudia Dräger had committed to providing every single item we had asked for, making this the largest single gift the company had given in its entire 150-year history.

A gift of such magnitude demands special recognition. As the precious equipment made its way via container to Peru, Claudia Dräger planned to travel with four employees for a formal presentation of this remarkable contribution. Four more Dräger employees arrived from Costa Rica and El Salvador to help prepare for this momentous occasion. To top it all, Mrs. Dräger had authorized the free installation of $50,000 worth of Dräger's own software on our hospital computers. Diospi Suyana would be the first hospital in South America to pilot this software program.

Tove Hohaus was elated. She had worked at the municipal clinic in Memmingen for five years, dreaming of, but never seeing, software such as this. Our anesthesiologist experienced once again that, with patience and faith in God, dreams could come true at Diospi Suyana.

On August 31, I picked up Claudia Dräger and her team at the airport in Cusco. Their departure from São Paulo had been delayed, so we had to rework a good bit of the schedule. We were able to make our scheduled social gathering with the rest of the Diospi Suyana staff that evening.

As everyone eyed the buffet, I told the Diospi Suyana chronicle one more time. Michael Karsta had already heard it, but his boss and colleagues had not. It was impossible to share the story without talking about my own search for God. The development of the hospital and the development of my faith were so intertwined that there simply was no separating one from the other. Then I asked Tove Hohaus and Michael Mörl to give a bit of their own testimony, which they both did gladly.

The next day, a Sunday, I gave the Dräger group a tour of the hospital. After lunch at our house, we visited some Indio families whom my wife was taking care of.

Then it was Monday. At 11 a.m., we invited the patients from the waiting room to the special event in the chapel. Claudia Dräger sat in the front row with the rest of the Dräger contingent. Hospital workers and Quechua Indios in national dress formed a colorful throng right behind them. A representative from the German Embassy in Peru, the second-largest Peruvian television network, and the local press were all also present for this momentous occasion.

Tina and I publicly recognized the Dräger gift as the largest Diospi Suyana had ever received. The state-of-the-art equipment, software, and service were worth upwards of $300,000. The formal ceremony included musical interludes and a traditional ribbon-cutting. After the ceremony, a group of about fifty Quechuas had their picture taken together with our guests from Dräger. They had really only just met, but now a bridge of generosity had made them friends.

Before they left on Monday afternoon, I put a bug in Claudia Dräger's ear that we would like to add a dental clinic to Diospi Suyana. All of Apurímac's 500,000 residents needed a dentist badly. Even young people had mouths that looked like neglected rock quarries or excavation sites. Almost everyone had missing or rotten teeth, and many suffered from chronic toothache.

I voiced this next chapter of my dream to a woman who had seen Diospi Suyana with her own eyes. I knew she had many contacts in international as well as German firms, and I hoped she might be willing to use those contacts on our behalf.

Throughout the next eight months, Claudia Dräger was able to orchestrate appointments for me with top business managers in several countries. As a result of her efforts, we were able to build and equip the dental clinic.

In October 2008, I met with a manager of the Sirona company in Austria. This resulted in the donation of three digital oral X-ray machines and five dentist's chairs, the total value of which was around $150,000. The Kavo Group furnished the entire clinic at a cost of $100,000 after I had met with Larry Culp, Director of Dannaher Inc. in Washington, for a single hour on March 2, 2009. At the beginning of May, I spoke to the CEO of Henry Schein in New York. Stanley Bergman represented the largest distributor of dental products in the entire world, and I will never forget the meeting with him at the Four Seasons Hotel in New York. There we were:

I HAVE SEEN GOD

him a Jew and me a German, him a Jew and me a Christian. As I shared my presentation I made no secret of where I came from or what I believed. The outcome was that Henry Schein donated $200,000 worth of materials for the clinic.

My own message at gatherings and celebrations related to the hospital is always the same. I tell of my fear of death, my often desperate search for God, and the many miracles that defy logic and mathematical probability several times over. Christians of all denominations can be encouraged to trust God anew. Even agnostics may be challenged into entertaining the notion that there might just be more to this life than we imagine after all.

53

Diospi Suyana Hospital Today

Anybody driving from Abancay towards Curahuasi can see the mission hospital down in the valley. From this vantage point 10,000 feet up, the red roofs and white walls blend into the landscape beautifully, and the dominant feature is the chapel with its striking silver cross.

Although it took almost a year of staggered department openings before Diospi Suyana was fully operational, 125,000 patients were treated there between October 2007 and June 2014. According to our statistics, 75 per cent of our patients speak Quechua, the language of the ancient Incas. Eighty per cent of them travel in from other Peruvian states, and 80 per cent of them fall into the category of extreme poverty, destitute by even Peruvian standards. In 2014, fifty-two missionaries were serving in Curahuasi, hand in hand with 110 local nationals, making Diospi Suyana the largest employer in the area.

With its abundant high-tech equipment, Diospi Suyana is without a doubt one of the most modern clinics in the entire country. There are quite a few special features that are essentially unheard of in other Peruvian hospitals. The juwi, Viessman, and Solvis companies have together donated a total of four complete sets of solar equipment which provide "green" energy to heat water and illuminate the hospital grounds.

We have an incinerator to dispose safely of infectious waste. Our contemporary satellite equipment facilitates the critical connection to the rest of the world by phone and internet. Four state-of-the-art operating rooms are fitted out on a par with the very best clinics in Lima. The radiology department with its CAT scanner and digital technology, plus the laboratory, enable staff to pinpoint patients' problems quickly and accurately so that comprehensive treatment may begin. The Diospi Suyana ICU is probably better equipped than that of any other hospital in the Peruvian highlands. Another unique asset is our physical therapy department, complete with fitness equipment, ultrasound, and infrared treatment. And the long-term benefit of the dental clinic for the whole region cannot be underscored enough. And these are just the medical/technical perks of Diospi Suyana.

Our mission hospital has also served very much as a role model for Peru by means of the loving care showered on all our patients. Nobody is discriminated against for any reason, certainly not race or social class. On the Pan-American Highway, the famous interstate that connects Lima and Cusco, there is a sign posted on the way to the hospital. It reads: "Diospi Suyana, a hospital seeking to share the love of Christ." That is truly our hearts' desire and our commitment to all people.

In February 2009, a sociologist from Lima spent four days interviewing patients about their experience at Diospi Suyana. Mirtha Valverde was permitted to move freely through the hospital and select interviewees at will. Without exception, all of the fifty-one patients to whom she spoke reported complete satisfaction with the medical care received at our facility. They all also, regardless of denominational background, spoke highly of the morning prayers held routinely in the chapel.

Some of them even said they had experienced God in a whole new way while here.

Diospi Suyana is not the gateway to heaven. Like every other hospital, we experience stress, strain, and shortfalls. We are always on the lookout for skilled, selfless volunteers from abroad and qualified staff from the local area. As we are in an area of extreme poverty, we will continue to depend on the faithful provision of monthly financial support from around the world. Inclusive of the voluntary service provided by missionaries, two-thirds of our monthly budget is financed via donations.

As I write these words, Señora Clorinda is fighting for her life in our ICU. Without the surgical intervention of Dr. Daniel Zeyse, acute peritonitis would have killed her much earlier. Her family members expressed their view in this way: "No matter what the outcome – without this hospital, our sister surely would have died long ago and with much greater suffering. Thank you, thank you, thank you!"

54

Our Most Loyal Friends

Reading this book might have led you to assume that Diospi Suyana is financed almost exclusively by very large companies. As of July 2014, approximately 180 companies had given major gifts, particularly gifts in kind, adding up to a total value of approximately $6.4 million. This is indeed an enormous sum. But our records also show that 50,000 individuals, from Europe and the US, have actually contributed a greater total amount: about $14.5 million. These were the souls who believed in our vision long before the corporate executives had ever heard of us. The hospital would have been built without the large company donations, but not without the faithfulness of the scout troops, housewives, laborers, retirees, and others who gave so sacrificially.

I would like to highlight one exceptional group of individuals. These are the 953 (as of July 2014) who have committed to regular monthly financial support. Whether they send fifty cents or fifty dollars, they are our most faithful friends – our sponsors. They shouldered the cost of building the hospital and now they sustain its daily operations. Their regular gifts have made it possible for thousands of Peruvians to obtain the medical care they so needed. The fund-raising events that private individuals have organized for Diospi Suyana are as varied as they are numerous. With their hard work and creative thinking, they have not only raised large sums of money but have also given generously of their time and of themselves. Jonas Haunschild, a physics student, tutored young children and sent all his earnings to Diospi Suyana. Andrea Heilmann of Dade Behring and her husband requested that guests at their wedding refrain from bringing personal gifts, and instead make a donation to the hospital. Christine Fleck of Kirchheimboladen baked huge quantities of granola to sell, and then turned over all the proceeds. Catholic carol singers hit the streets of Cadolzberg, and the scouts at Trossingen Baptist Church collected paper for recycling. It would take a second book to honor the efforts of all who have worked to bring the dream of Diospi Suyana to fruition.

55

Faith in the Media

At the beginning of the Diospi Suyana journey, Tina and I presented our vision to a group of journalists in Oestrich-Winkel. The intention was to discuss options for sharing our story in print and via television media in order to heighten awareness. Back then, although we had some pretty pictures and novel ideas, we had no solid, feasible marketing plan.

The media people were of no help. They were uncomfortable with the overarching theme of faith, which pervaded all of our presentations. In our world, scandal and sensationalism are what sells newspapers and keeps TV ratings high. Since God doesn't "sell," He is often left out of the media all together.

This story demonstrates the complete fallacy of such a position. Over 400 television and print reports around the world have accurately portrayed Diospi Suyana as a work of faith. Major German newspapers such as the *Frankfurter Allgemeine Zeitung*, the *Berliner Tagesspiegel*, and *Die Welt* have all published detailed reports on our mission. The *Hamburger Abendblatt*, the *Weser Kurier*, the *Hannoversche Allgemeine*, the *Reutlinger Generalanzeiger*, and many other smaller regional papers have also played their part in drawing the interest of the public to Diospi Suyana, sometimes including articles of a full page or more. Financial journals including *Forum MLP*, *Insurance Hösch*, and *Partner* have also introduced Diospi Suyana to thousands of readers.

DBMobil, the German railway circular, included a spot in their August 2007 edition, made available to nearly a million express train passengers. Pop magazines such as *Lisa*, *Freizeitpass*, *Bild der Frau*, and *Tina* have run feature articles multiple pages in length. The aptly named *Tina* alone is read by 3 million women. All this coverage by secular sources is in addition to those periodicals that one would actually expect to have an interest in our story: the medical and Christian (both Catholic and Protestant) publications.

Meanwhile, Diospi Suyana has become known in many countries via publications in the press or from TV productions. In November 2013 Deutsche Welle TV broadcast a twenty-six-minute report about our "hospital of hope" in several languages all around the world. The focus of that broadcast was the issue of faith.

Without exception, all these written accounts have clearly illustrated authentic faith and divine intervention, the results of which cannot be explained away by logic or science. My experience with journalists throughout Germany is that faith is worth writing about, if it can be done in a credible manner.

In the first half of 2009, the Peruvian–Chilean Neptunia Group invested $30,000 in the creation and distribution of a 160-page photo book. It chronicles the history of Diospi Suyana in three languages, and, by means of fascinating narrative, leaves no doubt that the glory of the mission hospital belongs to God. Freelance writer Alex Kornhuber, whose work has been featured in top international newspapers such as *The*

New York Times and *The Washington Post*, contributed 5,000 photos from his two visits to Curahuasi. Finally, in August, the popular glamor magazine *Cosas*, usually full of Hollywood gossip and socialite news, had six full pages dedicated to a most unusual subject: our mission hospital in the Andes. Over 50,000 corporate leaders, the movers and shakers of German society, learned about Diospi Suyana in the Rotary magazine just before Christmas 2009. The article was entitled "God, please work a miracle!"

In Peru, Diospi Suyana is known as *El Hospital de la Fe*, "The Hospital of Faith." It was the media who first dubbed the hospital as such, a very apt and appropriate sentiment, in my opinion. In a three page report for *Somos*, the most widely read Peruvian periodical, its star journalist Doris Bayly told her 1 million readers: "If faith can move mountains, in the John family's case, it can also shake wallets, transform hearts, and persuade authorities. This faith has overcome the mire of bureaucracy, deep-rooted skepticism, and even blunt rejection. It has circumvented blocked roads, blown mathematical arguments out of the water, and united Catholic and Protestant Christians in one love for God and fellow man."

56

A Direct Line to God

I don't know how many more years I have. That accident back in December 2008 reminded me that any day could very easily be my last. But when I look back on my life, I am exceedingly grateful. The vision my wife and I have shared has come to fruition in a way we could never have imagined even in our wildest dreams when we met thirty years ago. I have told the incredible story nearly 2,000 times in schools, universities, and clubs in 19 countries; shared it with high-powered executives, mass media, and men of the cloth. I know that people get goose bumps the first time they hear it. Quite frankly, I still do.

I don't know why God has chosen to show Himself so often and so clearly in our lives. Although His hand is in all things, sometimes His intervention is a bit more subtle, almost as if He wishes to remain anonymous. Maybe He took a different approach with me because I had doubted Him for so many years. He always seems to have a special plan for the doubters, the broken, and the desperate. I did always have an unrestrained desire to see and experience God.

My creed for the last thirty years is one shared by the apostle Paul, who wrote these words to a group of Christians in the city of Philippi: "I want to know (see) Christ, the power of His resurrection, and the fellowship of sharing in His sufferings, becoming like Him in His death, so as somehow to attain to the resurrection from the dead!" (Philippians 3:10–11).

Perhaps you view God as one option among many. When Jürgen Tritten was sworn in as Minister of the Environment in 1998, he was asked why he refused to utter the words "so help me God," typically included in an oath of office.

He replied, "Why should God help me now? He hasn't before!"

I have a different take on life. Everything I have, everything I am, has been given to me: a precious gift from God's almighty hand.

Without God, we can sit by the fire each evening and debate the meaning of life, but we will never reach a satisfactory conclusion.

Augustine, one of the wise men of the Christian faith, said long ago during the fourth century, "Our souls have no rest until they find their rest in God."

I have found fulfillment in communion with Christ. As long as I live, I want to follow Him and feel His presence.

On September 30, 2008, the *Hamburger Abendblatt* ran a report about me, entitled "The doctor with a direct line to God." This article was even mentioned on the official website of the Peruvian government. It sounds pretty extraordinary – a direct line to God. But it is in fact open to all who will let go and fall into His arms.

What God asks of us is unconditional faith in Him. Just mentally accepting that God exists isn't enough. If you can really mean it when you say these words from The Lord's Prayer, "Your will be done on earth as it is in heaven," then your heart is one He can mold, and you can be used to His greater glory and purpose. Over time, we see more and more clearly that our lives are a like a tapestry in which the threads of defeat, despair, and desperation all lend their colors to the beautiful design that emerges.

During a tour of the US back in May 2006, I met a man named Jonathan Sigworth in a rehabilitation center in New Haven, Connecticut. In February of that same year, he had been in India on a mission trip. While riding his bicycle, he suddenly went off the road and plunged over a fifty-foot drop. The impact broke his neck and resulted in permanent paralysis of all his limbs. He was taken to the nearest hospital, where he regained consciousness in the emergency room. He immediately realized his situation was grave, and asked the doctors whether or not he would ever be able to move his arms and legs again. They feared telling him the truth, and therefore said nothing.

Jonathan's response was completely unexpected.

"No matter whether I can walk in the future or not, I want my life to honor God."

Such words from a man whose dreams had just been shattered, whose plans had just been ripped away from him. As I stood before his bed, I sensed no bitterness, depression, or self-pity. His face was radiant and a deep sense of peace emanated from him.

Two years later, I gave Jonathan's father a call to see how he was doing.

"Has he ditched his faith in God?" I asked, anxious about the possible reply.

"Not at all. Jonathan has gone back to India, and right now he is working on a film to encourage the wheelchair-bound!"

I have no explanation for why God allowed this horrible accident to happen to Jonathan. But I am absolutely certain that He loves him, and me, and you, with an everlasting, boundless love. That is why Jesus died on the cross. When He was nailed to the beams, it was not the tragic conclusion of an earthly political drama. No; Christ came into this world with a purpose, to give His life for the sin of all mankind. At the cross, we are invited to come, to lay down our burdens, and to begin a new life in Him. That is why I personally believe that no other symbol expresses love more completely than the cross.

That is not the end of the good news. Through the resurrection, Jesus strengthens our faith that there is indeed something more than this world, a real life after our earthly death. Heaven isn't simply a consolation for facing death: it is a place where God's presence is very real; where there are no more tears, suffering, or death. It is for this hope that Christians throughout history have been willing to take risks, speak boldly, and even give up their life at the hands of those who would not believe.

Many of our volunteers have amazing personal stories to tell. I would like to end this book by sharing just one, from the life of Tove Hohaus. Tove grew up in former West Germany in very difficult circumstances. Her father abandoned the family. Although he made good money as a doctor, he refused to pay child support. As a result, Tove's mother had to work extremely hard just to provide the basic necessities for Tove and her brother. Family life was usually tense, money was tight, and sometimes there was nothing in the refrigerator. On top of these challenges, Tove suffered immensely from the realization that her own father had rejected her.

When Tove was ten years old, there was a big fight at home that sent her straight to the edge. Tove ran out of the apartment and towards the street, intending to throw herself in front of the first car that came along. Just at that moment, Tove heard a voice, loud and clear, behind her.

"I love you and I still have something for you to do!"

Tove looked around but could see no one, but she got the message: if someone loved her, her life was indeed worth living. From that moment on, Tove dedicated her life to that voice – the voice of God.

Jesus' outstretched arms, nailed to the cross, show the extent of God's love for you. Just as He offered His love to Tove, He offers it to you. With His strength, you can set a different course for your life and put your relationships right. If it is His will, you may find yourself implementing a great vision too – maybe even another hospital in Peru or in another corner of the world that longs to see the love of God delivered by the hands of the faithful.

What did the voice say to Tove? "I love you and I still have something for you to do."

If you would like to talk more with us about this, please contact us at www.diospi-suyana.de.

57

In Appreciation

I have already said that many, many people have contributed to the success of Diospi Suyana, more indeed than could ever be named here. But at this point I would like to express special thanks to a few key players.

Everything I am and do is largely the result of the influence of my parents, Wanda and Rudolf John. Their example, their faithfulness, and their support laid the foundation in my life for Diospi Suyana. (Sadly, my mother died in February 2010 and my father followed in March 2011.)

The same is true of my wife's parents. Hermann and Christa Schenk shaped Martina in such a way that I could not resist the temptation to marry her! They continue to support us as a missionary family in every way they can.

My sister Helga is our secret warrior in Wiesbaden. She attends to all the official paperwork in Germany, sends out our family newsletter, and flies to Peru to see us almost every year. My brother, Hartmut John, his wife, Mirjam, and my sister Gerlinde Bürger are friends I know I can always count on when the going gets tough.

Alongside my wife and me, Olaf Böttger is the third pillar of Diospi Suyana. For the past twelve years he has invested his evenings and weekends in the work. He, my wife, and I make all important decisions together. We are blessed by the entire Böttger family. Olaf's sister, Annette, is an auditor who oversees the foundation in her leisure time. His brothers have been regular financial supporters for years, and his parents are there, ready to help, any time a container needs packing. Rosemarie Böttger even mans the office when our office staff are on leave.

Many thanks are also due to the other members, who have shouldered this responsibility with us. They deserve to be named individually: Jürgen Eisenkolb, Heinrich Finger, Thomas Frehse, Gisela Graf, Udo and Barbara Klemenz, Dr. Wilfried and Dr. Marianne Knoll, Holger Krüger, Tobias and Judith Kühl, Martin and Ellen Nebel, Uwe, Ilse, and Karsten Schmiedicke, and Reinhard and Jeannette Zilz. In the US my heartfelt gratitude goes to Dr. Roger Smalligan, who serves as the President of Diospi Suyana USA. Steve Deters did a lot of paperwork to get us recognized as an official non-profit-organization by the IRS. Jim Miller invests his valuable time in acting as our current secretary. Another board member is surgeon Charly Ferguson. He invited me twice to the Massachusetts General Hospital in Boston to lecture before faculty members and Harvard medical students.

In many cities across Germany, there are individuals who have made extraordinary contributions to Diospi Suyana: the former chief editor of the *Reutlinger Generalanzeiger*, Christoph Irion and his wife, Dagmar; Rolf Nikel and (up to her death) his wife, Regine; Jakobus Schneider, Michael Spanner, and Mario Mayer, who invested 500 hours in the production of the Diospi Suyana film that has been seen by hundreds of thousands of people in Europe.

You may remember how, at the beginning of the book, I described meeting my wife at school. It has been her love, faithfulness, and loyalty and her untiring service that have made this story possible. If you maybe think of me as the engine of Diospi Suyana, then my wife is undoubtedly its heart and soul.

58

Our Team

On the day the clinic was inaugurated we had thirty missionaries at our mission station in Curahuasi, all but two from Germany. As Diospi Suyana has become better and better known, the team has developed into an international working group with more Americans, Canadians, Paraguayans and Dutch, etc. joining us each year, and as of 2014 there are twelve nations represented. The team language in the hospital, the Kids' Clubs and (from March) the Diospi Suyana School is Spanish.

Without the service of our long-term volunteer missionaries in Curahuasi, my wife and I would never have been able to build and operate the hospital. Our special thanks go to these friends who have been, and still are, willing to walk a stretch of the way with us in Peru:

Jörg and Birgit Bardy (Germany)

Bettina Baumgarten (Germany)

Ulrike Beck (Germany)

Yael Becker (Germany)

Christian and Verena Bigalke (Germany)

Hanna Böker (Germany)

Dr. David and Dr. Dorothea Brady (Austria/Germany)

Dr. Alex and Dr. Laura Brunner (USA, Tennessee)

Bärbel Bühler (Germany)

Cornelia Bühler (Switzerland)

Dr. Erin Connally (USA, Washington)

Dr. Ari Cale (USA, Oklahoma)

Dr. William and Allison Caire (USA, Texas)

Miriam Crisanto (Germany)

Markus Dirksen (Germany)

Oebele and Debora de Haan (Netherlands/ Germany)

Dr. Susan and Daniel Dreßler (Germany)

Lena Ehlebracht (Germany)

Dr. Oliver and Birgit Engelhard (Germany)

Dr. Renate Engisch (Germany)

Martin and Eva Friedli (Switzerland)

Dorothea Frölich (Germany)

Tabea Fröhlich (Germany)

Jana Füllbrandt (Germany)

Simon and Belen Giesbrecht (Argentina, Germany)

Dr. Annette Haar (Germany)

Dr. Jens and Damaris Hassfeld (Germany)

Ortrun Heinz (Germany)

Dana Henning (Germany)

Stefan and Petra Höfer (Germany)

Martin and Irmtraud Hoene (Germany)

Marion Hofmann (Germany)

Tove Hohaus (Germany)

Dominik and Katharina Hüttner (Germany)

Burkhard and Caroline Jochum (Germany)

Udo and Barbara Klemenz (Germany)

Carolin Klett (Germany)

Timo and Simone Klingelhöfer (Germany)

Alexandra Kopp (Germany)

Katrin Krägler (Germany)

John and Viola Lentink (Netherlands/Germany)

Esther Lietzau (Germany)

Dr. Heike Lindacher (Germany)

Bettina Markwart (Canada)

Lyndal Maxwell (Australia)

Tina Maria Metz (Germany)

Tibor and Stefanie Minge (Germany)

Dr. Kirsten and Ryan Morigeau (USA, Oregon)

Katharina Miske (Germany)

Michael and Elisabeth Mörl (Germany)

Carolin Müller (Germany)

Claudia Nikel (Germany)

Sarah Nafziger (Germany)

Dr. Frank and Anja Nöh (Germany)

Christian and Sabine Oswald (Germany)

Isabel Ott (Germany)

Patricia Piepiora (Germany)

Silvia Rojas (Germany)

Anna-Charlotta Rönnqvist (Finland)

Silvia Rojas (Peru)

Markus and Julianna Rolli (Switzerland)

Dr. Lutz and Christine Schoeneich (Germany)

Claudia Schultze (Germany)

Michael Schweitzer (Germany)

Stefan and Tabea Seiler (Germany)

Inessa Tews (Germany)

Tommy and Jessica Toews (Paraguay)

Sabine Vogel (Germany)

Erika Wall (Germany)

Gabriele Wall (Paraguay)

Lilli Warkentin (Germany)

Dr. John and Crystal Washburn (USA, Missouri)

Marit Weilbach (Germany)

Gerhard and Heike Wieland (Germany)

Alexandra Winter (Germany)

Nolan and Konica Wright (USA, Tennessee)

Dr. Stephen and Finley Wright (USA, Tennessee)

Dr. Daniel and Dr. Melanie Zeyse (Germany)

In addition to those who stayed for extended periods, there are those who came for a few weeks or months during their vacation. God is not limited by time, and, through these people, extraordinary things were accomplished.

I would like to give a special mention to Dr. David Brady. As former deputy director of the hospital, he has done great things and has spoken encouragement to me more than once when there were difficult decisions to be made. His role later fell to Dr. Jens Hassfeld, whose willingness to serve with his wife, Damaris, at our hospital for many years to come put me at ease about the destiny of Diospi Suyana in the event that I should die prematurely.

Sponsor Companies

The following companies and associations have sponsored equipment, consumer goods, transportation and fees for Diospi Suyana:

Abbott GmbH – anesthetic gases

Accuaproduct S.A.C. (Peru) – water purification equipment

Adifan – medicine

Aesculap AG & Co. KG – surgical instruments

Agfa HealthCare PACS – digitalization units

Albujar Médica (Peru) – centrifuges

Altendorf GmbH & Co. KG – circular saw

Alturas Minerals (Peru) – financial gifts

Andromeda Medizinische Systeme GmbH – urology equipment

Ascobloc Gastro-Gerätebau GmbH – kitchen appliances

Asociacíon Atocongo (Peru) – cement

B Braun, Melsungen (Germany/Peru) – surgical instruments, infusions, charity golf cup

Battery-direct-GmbH – USVs

Bauscher GmbH & Co. KG – vacuum cleaners

Baxterfinancial – gifts

Bild hilft e. V. – financial support for our school

Binderlaboratory – incubator

Bode – disinfectant

Boehringer Ingelheim – financial gifts, computer

Castrovirreyna (Peru) – financial gifts

CBMeye – surgery equipment

CIA des Minas Buenaventura (Peru)   financial gifts

Claro América Móvil Perú (Peru/Mexico) – telephone lines

CMA CGM – sea transportation

Cordillera de las Minas S.A. (Peru) – financial gifts

Corporación Aceros Arequipa S.A. (Peru) – steel

COVIDIEN Germany GmbH – pulsoximeter

Dade Behring Marburg GmbH – laboratory equipment

Deister Electronic – security system

Detroit Diesel mtu Perú s.a.c. (Peru) – emergency generator

Deutsche Pharma – medicine

DHL – transportation

Diveimport S.A. (Peru) – ambulances

Dorst Haulage GmbH – transportation

Dräger Werk AG & Co. KG – respirators, and much more

DT & Shop – materials for dental laboratory

Electro Sur Este (Peru) – light towers and more

Envirolab Perú (Peru) – water analysis

ERBE Elektromedizin GmbH – surgical equipment

Eudim – financial gifts

Fein – multi-master equipment

Fisher & Paykel Health Care (Germany/USA) – equipment for intensive care unit

Fresenius Medical Care Germany GmbH – financial gifts

Friends of the Indios in Peru – unimogs/pick-up trucks and other donations

German Army – uniforms for the hospital

Global Crossing (Peru/USA) – satellite equipment and fees

Haag-Streit International – slit lamp and an octopus perimetry machine

Hamburg Süd – sea transportation

Hawo GmbH – cutting and sealing equipment

HDG Safes – safe

Hegner GmbH – scroll saw

Heine – otoscopes and stethoscopes

Helmut Hund GmbH – microscopes

Helvex Peru S.A. (Mexico) – water faucets

Henry Schein (Germany/USA) – equipment for dental clinic

Hermann Flörke GmbH – financial gifts and advertising material

Hissin Medizintechnik GmbH – defibrillators

Hochschild Mining PLC (Peru) – financial gifts

Horn – kitchen appliances

Humedica – furniture and other gifts in kind

HWK Medizintechnik – physical therapy benches

Indeco S.A. (Peru/Chile) – cables

Inka GmbH – financial gifts

Inotec Company – financial gifts

Jansen & Buscher GmbII & Co. KG – lead profiles for stained-glass windows

JHS (Peru) – gynecology chair

Johann M.K. Blumenthal GmbH – financial gifts

Johnson & Johnson MEDICAL GmbH – suture material

Josfel Illuminación (Peru) – lamps

juwi solar GmbH – photovoltaic equipment

Kaltenbach – workshop

Kärcher – steam cleaner

Karl Storz – laparoscopy equipment

Katadyn (Switzerland/Germany) – water filters

Kavo Dental GmbH – dental furnishings

KCI Medizinprodukte GmbH – vacuum system and accessories

Kieback & Peter – office furnishings

Klaus Koch Printers GmbH – printing products

KLS Martin Group – operating room lights and RF device

Kodra Walter Fischer GmbH & Co. – bedpan flushers

Kossodo S.A.C. (Peru) – microscope

Kreussler Pharma – antibiotics and cleaning fluids

Lautenschläger GmbH & Co. KG – sterilizing equipment

Leica Microsystems Weilburg – microscope

Lohse and Schilling GmbH – installation of computers

Macromedica S.A. (Peru) – furniture

Mainmetall – accessories for solar equipment

Manuel Centeno Martino (Peru) – financial gifts for printing products

Maquet – patient transporters

McCann Erickson – financial gifts for printing products

MDH-Perforación Diamantina (Peru) – steel, cement, well construction

Medifarma (Peru) – medication

Melag – sterilizing equipment

Metax (Peru) – furniture

Miele – washing machine and drier

Miyasato (Peru) – window panes

Nefusac Negociación Futura S.A.C. (Peru) – tiling accessories

Neptunia S.A. (Peru) – transportation, storage, book

Nora systems – floor coverings for our school

Oberle Foundation – financial gift for windows

Olympus (Germany/Japan) – endoscopy equipment

On site Gas Systems (USA) – oxygen generators

Pacífico Seguros (Peru) – auto insurance

Paul Hartmann AG – bandages and more

Pentax (Germany/Japan) – endoscopes

Peri – frame work material

Philips – ultrasound scanners, CHG unit

Radiometer Medical ApS (Denmark) – blood gas apparatus and reagents

Relius – paint

Richard Wolf GmbH – endoscopy equipment

Roche (Switzerland) – lab equipment and reagents

Rudolf Riester GmbH & Co. KG – laryngoscopes and more

Sandoz (Germany/Switzerland) – financial gifts and medication

Sanitär-Heinze Trading Co. – accessories for heating system

Schenck Technologie & Industriepark – storage and packing

Schmitz & Sons – operating tables and furnishings

Schölly – laparoscopy tower

Schott AG – stained glass for chapel windows

Schülke & Mayr GmbH – disinfectant

SENSUM Graphics – graphics work

Siemens Medical Solutions – computer tomogram

Sirona Dental GmbH – digital X-ray equipment and dental chairs

Sistema Analíticos (Peru) – lab equipment

Solvis GmbH & Co. KG – solar equipment

Southern Peru (Peru/Chile) – roof plates and cables

Stengelin Paul Medical GmbH – surgical instruments

Stoss Medica – medical equipment

Streck Transport – transportation

Sulo – trash containers

TecnoMedis (Peru) – internal fittings of ambulances

Trebol Celima (Peru/Belgium) – tiles

Tresor TEC – safe

Ulrich GmbH & Co. KG (Switzerland) – infusion pumps

UroVision – urology materials

Viessmann – solar equipment

Wilde Medizin-Technik – operating theater lighting

Wissner-Bosserhoff – mattresses

WPO – equipment for the handicraft room of our school

ZOLL Medical Germany GmbH – defibrillators

The John Family, June 2014

Diospi Suyana – "We trust in God"

HEART OF THE GOSPEL

Sermon Notes of Rev John Maciver and Rev John Mackenzie

Edited by Iain D Campbell

Christian Focus Publications

Dedicated to the memory of my grandparents,
John and Anne Mackenzie,
and Donald and Peggy Campbell,
who, having served their generation by the will of God,
fell asleep in Jesus.

© 1995 Iain D. Campbell
ISBN 1-85792-182-8

Published by
Christian Focus Publications Ltd.
Geanies House, Fearn, Ross-shire,
IV20 1TW, Scotland, Great Britain.